T0360491

Management and Industry

This shortform book presents key peer-reviewed research selected by expert series editors and contextualised by new analysis from each author on how the specific field addressed has evolved.

With contributions on the 'historic turn' in management studies, workers' rights, occupational health, industrial networks and the development of the organisation, practices and principles of large UK businesses, this volume provides an array of fascinating insights into industrial history.

Of interest to business and economic historians, this shortform book also provides analysis and illustrative case-studies that will be valuable reading across the social sciences.

John F. Wilson is Pro Vice-Chancellor (Business and Law) at Northumbria University at Newcastle. He has published widely in the fields of business, management and industrial history, including ten monographs, six edited collections and over seventy articles and chapters. Most notably, his *British Business History, 1720–1994* is still being used in UK universities. He was also the founding editor of the *Journal of Industrial History*, as well as co-editor of *Business History* for ten years.

Nicholas D. Wong is Vice-Chancellor's Senior Research Fellow at Newcastle Business School, Northumbria University. His research areas cover historical organisation studies and uses of the past, family business studies and entrepreneurship. He has published in *Business History, International Journal of Contemporary Hospitality Management* and *Entreprise et Histoire*. Nicholas won the John F. Mee Best Paper Award at the Academy of Management in 2018 for his contribution to the Management History Division.

Steven Toms spent fifteen years in senior management at Nottingham University as head of the undergraduate programme, chair of teaching committee and research director before becoming Head of York Management School in 2004. Professor Toms's research interests cover the role of accounting, accountability and corporate governance in the development of organisations, particularly from a historical perspective. He is interested in perspectives that integrate financial models with economic and organisational theory and corporate strategy. Specific applications range from business history – in particular cotton and other textiles trades – to capital markets and social and environmental accounting. He was editor of the journal *Business History* from 2007 to 2013.

Routledge Focus on Industrial History
Series Editors: John F. Wilson, Nicholas D. Wong and Steven Toms

This shortform series presents key peer-reviewed research originally published in the *Journal of Industrial History*, selected by expert series editors and contextualised by new analysis from each author on how the specific field addressed has evolved.

Of interest to business historians, economic historians and social scientists interested in the development of key industries, the series makes theoretical and conceptual contributions to the field, as well as providing a plethora of empirical, illustrative and detailed case-studies of industrial developments in Britain, the United States and other international settings.

Published titles in this series include:

Growth and Decline of American Industry
Case Studies in the Industrial History of the USA
Edited by John F. Wilson, Nicholas D. Wong and Steven Toms

Management and Industry
Case Studies in UK Industrial History
Edited by John F. Wilson, Nicholas D. Wong and Steven Toms

Banking and Finance
Case Studies in the Development of the UK Financial Sector
Edited by John F. Wilson, Nicholas D. Wong and Steven Toms

Management and Industry

Case Studies in UK Industrial History

Edited by
John F. Wilson, Nicholas D. Wong
and Steven Toms

Routledge
Taylor & Francis Group

LONDON AND NEW YORK

First published 2020
by Routledge
2 Park Square, Milton Park, Abingdon, Oxon OX14 4RN

and by Routledge
52 Vanderbilt Avenue, New York, NY 10017

Routledge is an imprint of the Taylor & Francis Group, an informa business

British Library Cataloguing-in-Publication Data
A catalogue record for this book is available from the British Library

Library of Congress Cataloging-in-Publication Data
A catalog record for this book has been requested

ISBN: 978-0-367-02410-9 (hbk)
ISBN: 978-0-429-39977-0 (ebk)

Typeset in Times New Roman
by Apex CoVantage, LLC

Contents

Contributors

Michael Rowlinson Michael Rowlinson is Professor of Management and Organisational History at the University of Exeter, UK.

Geoffrey Tweedale Geoffrey Tweedale was Professor of Business History at Manchester Metropolitan University Business School. Then he developed an interest in the history of industrial hazards and *Magic Mineral to Killer Dust: Turner & Newall and the Asbestos Hazard* – the first study of a British asbestos company – was published by Oxford University Press in 2000 (2nd edition, 2001). A follow-up volume with Jock McCulloch, *Defending the Indefensible* (OUP, 2008), explored the global asbestos disaster. It was awarded the Wadsworth Prize by the Business Archives Council in 2009.

John Quail John Quail received his external doctorate in business history from Leeds University in 1996. He has never held an academic post, not for the want of trying but applications for first academic posts when you are the same age as the head of department will never go very well. He has contributed to a number of business history journals and edited compilations. In retirement he has been appointed a Visiting Fellow in York Management School.

Andrew Popp Andrew Popp is Professor of History at Copenhagen Business School. He is Editor-in-Chief of *Enterprise and Society*.

Introduction

*John F. Wilson, Nicholas D. Wong
and Steven Toms*

Purpose and significance of the series

The concept of the *Routledge Series of Industrial History* was motivated by the desire of the editors to provide an outlet in the public domain for articles originally published in the now cancelled *Journal of Industrial History* (*JIH*). By utilising an extensive repository of top-quality publications, the series will ensure that the authors' findings will be able to contribute to recent debates in the field of management and industrial history. The articles contained in these volumes will appeal to a wide audience, including business historians, economic historians and social scientists interested in longitudinal studies of the development of key industries and themes. Moreover, the series will provide fresh insight into how the academic field has developed in the last twenty years.

The editors believe that the quality of scholarship evident in the articles originally published in the *JIH* now deserve a much broader audience. The peer-reviewed articles are built on robust business-historical research methodologies and are subject to extensive primary research. The series will make important theoretical and conceptual contributions to the field, as well as providing a plethora of empirical, illustrative and detailed case-studies of industrial developments in Britain, the United States and other international settings. The collection will be of interest to a broad spectrum of social scientists, and especially business school and history department academics, as they provide valuable case-study material that can be used in both teaching and research.

Building on the original *Journal of Industrial History* journal

The first edition of the *Journal of Industrial History* was published in 1998 with the aim of providing 'clear definitional parameters for industrial historians' and, in turn, establishing links between 'industrial history and theoretical work in social science disciplines like economics, management (including international business), political science, sociology, and anthropology'. As it is over twenty years since its original publication, it is clear that the relevance of the *JIH* has stood the test of time. The original *JIH* volumes covered a diverse range of topics including: industrial structure and behaviour, especially in manufacturing and services; industrial and business case-studies; business strategy and structure; nationalisation and privatisation; globalisation and competitive advantage; business culture and industrial development; education, training and human resources; industrial relations and its institutions; the relationship between financial institutions and industry; industrial politics, including the formulation and impact of industrial and commercial policy; and industry and technology. The current *Routledge Series of Industrial History* will provide a cross-section of articles that cover a wide range of themes and topics, many of which remain central to management studies. These include separate volumes covering 'management and industry'; 'industry in the USA'; and 'banking and finance'. Future volumes in the series will cover 'case-studies in British industrial history'; 'technology'; and 'cotton and textile industry'. The *Routledge Series of Industrial History* will reframe highly original material that illustrates a wide variety of themes in management and organisation studies, including entrepreneurship, strategy, family business, trust, networks and international business, focusing on topics such as growth of the firm, crisis management, governance, management and leadership.

Contribution and key findings of the chapters in Volume One

The current volume is focused on the theme of 'management and industry', including articles that examine organisation theory and management strategies in UK industry over the period 1850–1958. The volume contains two chapters by Rowlinson and by Quail that provide new theoretical frameworks which contribute to an improved understanding of the connection between business history and organisational theory and the evolution of UK management structures. The chapters by Tweedale and by Popp provide case-studies of management issues in different UK industrial sectors. To explain in a little more detail, Rowlinson's chapter provides an innovative theoretical lens through which business historians can connect their work with the field of organisation theory. Quail's chapter sheds fresh light on industrial history by providing a new approach to

Chandlerian business-historical approaches, with the development of the concept of a 'proprietorial theory'. Tweedale provides an historical case-study that provides a 'bottom-up', or 'history from below', perspective of workers' rights and human resource management. Popp's chapter provides an historical perspective on an important area of industrial history in terms of its focus on networks and trust in the Potteries.

The first chapter, 'Business history and organization theory', is a study by Michael Rowlinson that was part of a wider project that sought to introduce the 'historic turn' in management studies. The original paper in context was written in response to increasing numbers of business historians finding employment in business schools, calling for a shift away from the purely empirical and positivist historical studies to a more theoretical basis of business-historical enquiry. Emerging from this debate was a subsequent article, co-authored by Rowlinson, which featured in *Business History* in 2004: 'The treatment of history in organisation studies: Towards an 'historic turn'?' (Clark & Rowlinson, 2004), which today is the most cited article to feature in that journal. The paper makes two important contributions: the first examines the links between business history and organisation theory, moving beyond the simple borrowing of models from sociology and economics and challenging the 'ahistorical nature of theories of organisations'; the second calls for a distinction between the theorised field of 'business history' and narrative 'company histories'. This influential article laid the foundation for a torrent of research that considered the role of business historians in management schools and the use of business-historical research methodologies in broader branches of management studies such as entrepreneurship, strategy, international business and institutional theory. Recently the emergence of the 'uses of the past' field (Wadhwani, Suddaby, Mordhorst, & Popp, 2018) with related topics such as rhetorical history strategies (Suddaby & Greenwood, 2005; Suddaby, Foster, & Trank, 2010; Suddaby & Foster, 2016; Maclean, Harvey, Sillince, & Golant, 2018), the value of the corporate archive (Jones & Cantelon, 1993; Lipartito, 2014) and the corporate use of the archive (Donzé & Smith, 2018) have opened new opportunities for business historians and added value to the function of business history in management studies (Bucheli & Wadhwani, 2014).

The second chapter, 'Management strategies for health: J. W. Roberts and the Armley Asbestos Tragedy, 1920–1958' by Geoffrey Tweedale, provides a case-study that utilises extensive archival material to examine 'dangerous trades', revealing a 'history from below' perspective on workers' rights and occupational health. Especially novel in this chapter is the focus on how the deaths of workers influenced both the management strategies of the firm and government health and safety regulation. This study provides a pre-cursor to contemporary management scholarship on governance, the role of directors and develops insights into the emerging function of human resource management. Above all, it is apparent from Tweedale's research that there were institutional failures at numerous levels: failure of management at J. W. Roberts to safeguard adequately workers' health and wellbeing with, for example, appropriate dust safety and extraction processes; failure of government and regulatory bodies to adopt appropriate levels of legislation, medical surveillance and health and safety regulations; failure of the factory inspectorate to prosecute or censure J. W. Roberts for its unwillingness to comply with regulations; and failure to provide adequate levels of compensation to victims and families via the Industrial Industries Act and Workman's Compensation Act. It is an excellent case-study and pre-cursor into what has developed in the last twenty years into the field of human resource management and employee rights and welfare.

The third chapter by John Quail, 'The proprietorial theory of the firm and its consequences', examines the role of joint stock companies in developing the organisation, practices and principles of large UK businesses. Quail called these organisational principles the 'proprietorial theory of the firm', setting out a clear distinction between proprietor and manager, as well as between shareholder and director, which contains elements of classic agency theory (Eisenhardt, 1989; Laffont & Martimort, 2002; Rutherford, Springer, & Yavas, 2005; Zellweger & Kammerlander, 2015). The article establishes how the rigidity and inadaptability of UK management structures contributed to relative economic decline in the twentieth century, while at the same time outlining how the development of UK managerial structures failed to follow the Chandlerian managerialist framework. Building on this, a more recent study by Wilson, Buchnea, and Tilba (2018) provided fresh insights into the relationship between investors, ownership and directors by examining the complexity of the British corporate network between 1904 and 1976.

The final chapter in the volume, 'Trust in an industrial district: The Potteries, c.1850–1900' by Andrew Popp, provides insights into the nature of trust networks in the North Staffordshire potteries industry in the second half of the nineteenth century. In particular, it examines the changing degrees of trust in accordance with the Casson model (1990), uncovering the degree to which varying levels of trust within the industrial network helped improve performance and productivity. Importantly, the chapter provides insight into the growing tensions between large and small firms within the industry, foreshadowing recent scholarship on legitimacy. Popp uncovers the dichotomy between trust and collaboration on the one hand, and the pressures of competition and performance within industrial clusters on the other.

Conclusion

It is apparent from this brief review of the chapters that the first volume in the series makes important contributions to the field of industrial history in several ways. Firstly, it provides a series of high calibre and unique studies in aspects of industrial history that contribute to more recent debates on trust, legitimacy, industrial relations and human resource management. Secondly, the chapters shed light on studies that pioneered the link between history, business history and management studies generally. Finally, the volume provides strong historical case-studies that can be used by students and researchers who are exploring issues related to the evolution and development of UK management structures and industrial clusters. The editors believe that this volume will not only provide a much wider audience for articles that link into a wide range of topical issues, but also feed into debates in the wider social sciences. These are themes that will be developed further in subsequent volumes of the *Routledge Series of Industrial History*, highlighting the intrinsic value in republishing material from the *Journal of Industrial History* and ensuring that the articles contribute extensively to current debates.

References

Bucheli, M., & Wadhwani, R. D. (Eds.). (2014). *Organizations in time: History, theory, methods*. Oxford: Oxford University Press on Demand.

Casson, M. (1990). The economics of trust: Explaining differences in corporate structures between the US and Japan. In M. Casson (Ed.), *Enterprise and competitiveness: A systems view of international business* (pp. 105–124). Oxford: Oxford University Press.

Clark, P., & Rowlinson, M. (2004). The treatment of history in organisation studies: Towards an "historic turn"? *Business History*, 46(3), 331–352.

Donzé, P.-Y., & Smith, A. (2018). Varieties of capitalism and the corporate use of history: The Japanese experience. *Management & Organizational History*, 13(3), 236–257.

Eisenhardt, K. (1989). Agency theory: An assessment and review. *Academy of Management Review*, 14(1), 57–74.

Jones, A. A., & Cantelon, P. L. (1993). *Corporate archives and history: Making the past work*. Malabar, FL: Krieger Publishing.

Laffont, J.-J., & Martimort, D. (2002). *The theory of incentives: The principal-agent model*. Princeton, NJ: Princeton University Press.

Lipartito, K. (2014). Historical sources and data. In M. Bucheli & R. D. Wadhwani (Eds.), *Organizations in time: History, theory, methods* (pp. 284–304). Oxford: Oxford University Press.

Maclean, M., Harvey, C., Sillince, J. A. A., & Golant, B. D. (2018). Intertextuality, rhetorical history and the uses of the past in organizational transition. *Organization Studies, 39*(12), 1733–1755.

Rutherford, R., Springer, T., & Yavas, A. (2005). Conflicts between principals and agents: Evidence from residential brokerage. *Journal of Financial Economics, 76*, 627–665.

Suddaby, R., & Foster, W. M. (2016). History and organizational change. *Journal of Management, 43*, 19–38.

Suddaby, R., Foster, W. M., & Trank, C. Q. (2010). Rhetorical history as a source of competitive advantage. In J. A. C. Baum & J. Lampel (Eds.), *Advances in strategic management: The globalization of strategy research* (pp. 147–173). Bingley, UK: Emerald.

Suddaby, R., & Greenwood, R. (2005). Rhetorical strategies of legitimacy. *Administrative Science Quarterly, 50*, 35–67.

Wadhwani, R. D., Suddaby, R., Mordhorst, M., & Popp, A. (2018). History as organizing: Uses of the past in organization studies: Introduction. *Organization Studies, 39*(12), 1663–1683.

Wilson, J. F., Buchnea, E., & Tilba, A. (2018). The British Corporate Network, 1904–1976: Revisiting the finance-industry relationship. *Business History, 60*(6), 779–806.

Zellweger, T., & Kammerlander, N. (2015). Family, wealth, and governance: An agency account. *Entrepreneurship: Theory & Practice, 39*(6), 1281–1303.

Chapter 1

Business history and organization theory

Michael Rowlinson

There is a growing consensus among business historians that they need to engage with the theoretical concerns from related fields[1] if they are to refute the familiar criticism that they are '"inveterate empiricists", obsessed with setting the record straight, telling the story as it really was'.[2] In this article I want to examine the implications for business history of entering into a dialogue with organization theory. I hope that this will shed some light on the general dilemmas facing business history if it is to become more theoretical. Inevitably my impressions of business history reflect my own experience of historical research, my background in organizational sociology, and my interest in inter-disciplinary debate in organization theory.[3]

There is no easy way to define organization theory. It can be said to consist of 'clusters of research programmes held together by the discourse of specific communities of theorists with overlapping interests'.[4] Each community of theorists has its own criteria for deciding what constitutes organization theory. Some sociologists, like myself, tend to see it as being characterised by paradigm diversity, if not paradigm incommensurability.[5] But toleration of alternative paradigms is anathema to economists, who see themselves as the bearers of an 'incipient new science of organization' which will eventually subsume organization theory under a dominant economic paradigm.[6]

In considering the potential for dialogue between organization theory and business history I want to explore two themes. One theme is the possibility of business historians having a genuine engagement with organization theory by being able to choose between alternative paradigms, and also by contributing a historical perspective to the debates within and between paradigms. This challenges the implicitly accepted view that in order to become more theoretical it is sufficient for business historians to be passive recipients of theory from economics or sociology.

In addition to overcoming the atheoretical stance of business history, a genuine engagement should also highlight the ahistorical nature of most theories of organization.[7] The other theme is the different implications that alternative perspectives in organization theory have for the narrative company case studies that have hitherto been a mainstay of business history. In my view there is a danger that a more explicitly theoretical orientation may lead to an increased separation of theorised 'business history' from narrative 'company history'.

Given the impossibility of reviewing the whole gamut of organization theory I have chosen to structure this article around the three most prominent discourses that hold the major research programmes together.[8] The first of these discourses is organizational economics, which is concerned with reconciling economic theory with the existence of organizations. This brings together a family of concepts ranging from repeated games, property rights, principal and agent relationships, and transaction costs, through to evolutionary and resource based views of the firm.[9] I will focus on transaction cost economics and the advance of economic imperialism. The second discourse, organizational sociology, is concerned with the competing views of change in organizations, from structural contingency, institutional, ecological, and strategic choice perspectives.[10] Finally, the discourse of organizational culture, which is partly derived from anthropology, focuses on the meanings that organizations have for their members.[11] I will take this discourse to be comprised of three levels of analysis: corporate culturism, organizational symbolism, and post-modernism.

Organizational economics

Business historians know only too well that the so-called 'theory of the firm' in neoclassical economics is 'not a theory of the firm at all'.[12] It treats the firm as a 'black box',[13] and extreme versions of evolutionary market selection in economics leave little scope for the study of purposive behaviour in individual firms.[14] But economists claim that as a result of various developments in the theory of the firm, economics now has 'more to offer business historians than ever before'.[15] Some business historians have welcomed these developments, especially transaction cost economics and the resource based view of the firm, which build on the work of Coase and Penrose respectively.[16]

It could be argued that the resource based view of the firm allows most scope for a historical dimension because of its emphasis on the importance of path dependence. This leads to a view that the development of certain resources and capabilities by a firm depends upon a unique series of events in the firm's history.[17] But as yet the resource based view of the firm has had little impact in business history compared to transaction cost economics.[18] Furthermore, the resource based view of the firm has had more impact on the study of corporate strategy than it has in organization theory, whereas transaction cost economics is almost synonymous with an economic perspective in organization theory. Although this does not mean that the resource based view of path dependence has escaped criticism from organizational sociologists for its emphasis on change as an evolutionary process rather than the outcome of conflicts and dilemmas in organizations,[19] which should concern business historians interested in the internal politics of companies.

Given the prominence of transaction cost economics I will rehearse some of the criticisms that can be levelled against it from both historical and sociological perspectives before considering organizational economics in general as a manifestation of economic imperialism and the implications of this for business history.

Transaction cost economics

It is claimed that transaction cost economics 'subscribes to the proposition that history matters'. The importance of history in transaction cost economics has at least three dimensions. First, it is recognised that situations change over time. For example, a large number of suppliers may compete prior to a transaction. But once one or a few suppliers have made significant investments in assets that are specific to the transaction, the situation is transformed to one of a small number of suppliers who may enter into a bilateral relationship with buyers. Second, it is acknowledged that 'Tacit knowledge and its consequences' are important. Finally, it is accepted that 'The entire institutional environment (laws, rules, conventions, norms, etc.) within which the institutions of governance are embedded is the product of history.'[20]

The statement that 'history matters' might be taken to mean that the compatibility of business history and transaction cost economics is assured. But there are several reasons for treating such a statement with caution. In the first place the statement needs to be qualified with the rider that it does not 'imply that only history matters'. This allows for a critique of path dependence, which is relegated to a subordinate role whereby it merely delays efficient outcomes.[21] When it comes to important issues of organizational form the disregard for history in transaction cost economics is revealed. Thus it is maintained that it was 'Not by history but by logic' that the owners of capital became the owners of enterprise,[22] and the explanation and justification for the existence of conglomerates 'relies on a combination of *a priori* theorizing and related natural selection considerations.'[23] What is more, the broad 'set of consideration related to the history, religion, and culture of societies', upon which the enforcement of property rights depends,[24] tends to be taken as given in transaction cost economics as it is generally in organizational economics.[25]

When assessing the statement that 'history matters' it needs to be remembered that 'history' is an ambiguous term. Coase has pointed out that the unreal world of equilibrium and perfect competition, which is so readily susceptible to mathematical analysis, is also a world to which it is difficult to apply a meaningful concept of *time*.[26] However the acceptance that temporal or spatial dimensions need to be incorporated into explanations for the existence of particular organizational forms, does not necessarily require or justify empirical historical research into the origins of those organizational forms. If the logic of history can be explained satisfactorily in theoretical terms, then there is no need to refer to the narration of what has happened, except for the purposes of illustration. Organizational economics can be seen as an advance on the neoclassical theory of the firm, which does not account for time. But a theoretical account of the importance of time does not necessarily entail a sociological or historical interpretation of actual events.

A good example of economists' preference for 'hypothetical' as opposed to 'actual history',[27] and their questionable treatment of historical data is the transaction costs analysis of work organization.[28] Transaction cost economics imposes a logical progression on history, from the least to the most efficient modes of work organization. But historically insignificant modes of work organization are included in this progression simply because they are logically possible.[29]

Transaction cost economics can also be criticised for failing to offer any explanation of the 'causal process' whereby one form of organization arises and replaces another.[30] The 'inability to deal with process'[31] means that organizational and technological innovation is exogenized in transaction cost economics in much the same way that it is in mainstream neoclassical economics. Organizational sociologists have contrasted the neglect of 'volition' in the version of transaction cost economics that prevails in organization theory with alternative transaction cost approaches in economic history which take account of the importance of actors' competing pictures of the future, their 'subjective models', in relation to innovation.[32]

The Panglossian assumption that 'Whatever is, is efficient',[33] makes organizational economics vulnerable to the criticism that it is tautological.[34] As a result, organizational sociologists have characterised transaction cost economics in particular and organizational economics in general as 'efficiency theory', which neglects power, as well as social and political processes, in favour of explaining organizations solely in terms of cost minimisation.[35] The assumption in transaction cost economics that 'whatever organizational form is most efficient will be the one observed'[36] has been censured by sociologists for its implicit 'optimistic functionalism', by which they mean 'a mode of explanation whereby outcomes are attributed their beneficial consequences.'[37]

While functionalism is a feature of the discourse of organizational economics, it is less in evidence in alternative economic accounts of organization. For example, power is seen as ubiquitous in capitalist firms in neo-Marxian contested exchange theory.[38] Although contested exchange theory is no less economic in its approach than transaction cost economics,[39] mainstream economists can usually be relied upon not to mention it when giving an account of organizational economics for other organization theorists.[40]

Economic imperialism

Having modified the theory of the firm in order to account for the existence of formal economic organization and various features of it, economists then propose that their preferred 'theoretical framework should be adopted by business historians'.[41] But I want to caution business historians against adopting any particular economic theoretical framework on the grounds that this is likely to lead to the subordination of business history to economics. In the first place it should be borne in mind that the neoclassical paradigm dominates economics to such an extent that organizational economists are apt to make too much of their departures from the strictest neoclassical assumptions.[42] From the viewpoint of organizational sociologists, organizational economics remains rooted in rational choice theory and methodological individualism that are hallmarks of the neo-classical paradigm.[43] Organizational economics is also committed to the same deductive methodology as neoclassical economics. These characteristics mean that organizational economics can be seen as part of the imperialistic expansion of the economics.

Economists and their sympathisers in business history might object to the characterisation of organizational economics as imperialistic. Transaction cost economists claim that there is a 'healthy tension' involving a 'genuine give-and-take' between organizational economics and organizational sociology.[44] And in their overtures to business history, economists claim that they have changed their ways and that they no longer 'see business historians as research assistants for economists who engage in a higher level of thinking.'[45] But I am not arguing that economic imperialism derives from the imperious personalities of particular economists. Besides, even if they come in the guise of missionaries rather than conquistadors, economists still see themselves as bringing 'reason' to us savages in the primitive social sciences and humanities.

The imperialistic pronouncements of economists,[46] especially in the manifestos for organizational economics,[47] can be cited as evidence of their expansionist ambitions. Economic theorists readily admit that they 'are by nature system-builders'.[48] According to economists, 'In the best of all possible worlds' they would be able to 'present a fully integrated model of organizational economics'.[49] They aspire to 'supply a unifying framework of analysis for social science as a whole'.[50] And as far as many economists are concerned, 'organizational economics and organizational theory are (already) one and the same thing'.[51]

Economists are convinced that the social sciences should emulate an outdated model of the physical sciences by constructing a unified general theory. Their aim is to develop a general theory that can be applied to any and all situations. Thus transaction costs have been used to explain sexual reproduction[52] and political institutions,[53] as well as economic organization. As an organizational sociologist has remarked, the wide scope of such general theory 'does not usually lead economists to "visit with" other disciplines'.[54]

The implication of theory construction in economics is that all theoretical utterances in the social sciences should be reconciled with a unified general theory, and economists are rigorously trained in the analytical skills required to police the social sciences for irreconcilable statements. This leaves no room for paradigm diversity. Unless a historian is prepared to indulge in a deductive exercise to demonstrate the superior logic of one economic theory of organization over another, in other words to become an economist, then he or she has no criteria for choosing between economic theories that would satisfy an economist. If a historian chooses, say, a functional efficiency theory, such as transaction cost economics, over a theory of power, such as contested exchange, then this is likely to be an expression of mainstream rather than radical political sympathies and a concomitant faith in the intellectual superiority of favoured theorists.

The methodology of economics leaves little room for any contribution from the detailed historical case studies produced by business historians:

> Economists spend a lot of time worrying whether their metaphors – they call them 'models' – meet rigorous standards of logic. They worry less whether their stories – they call them 'stylized facts', a phrase that makes tiresome trips to the library unnecessary – meet rigorous standards of fact.[55]

This methodology can be discerned from the format of papers written by organizational economists. In the first place some phenomenon of interest is selected, for example the trite suggestion 'that managers who trust their employees obtain better results than those who do not'.[56] The evidence for this need be no more than 'anecdotal', a newspaper article that caught the economist's eye might suffice, but a detailed case study is certainly not required. This is followed by a list of assumptions that would need to be made in order to construct a model of an imaginary world in which the said phenomenon would result from the actions of self interested rational actors.

Economists have claimed that 'business history can offer economists useful correctives and provocative examples that will inspire them to give their models heightened realism and greater practical significance.'[57] But in practice the models proposed in organizational economics retain sufficient residual variables, such as 'atmosphere' or 'culture', to allow economic theorists to dismiss case study findings that are not to their liking.[58] So it must be asked what the consequences for business history would be of adopting a theoretical framework from organizational economics. For one thing, it would allow the functional logic of efficiency theory to be superimposed on to the narratives of business historians.[59] But this sort of *ex post* rationalisation constitutes a form of 'story telling' that has very little claim to scientific status in economics.[60] It confirms the suspicion that almost anything can be rationalised by invoking transaction costs. It would also reinforce the 'teleology, determinism, and functionalism'[61] that is a feature of the prevailing interpretation of the rise of the modern corporation in business history, which radical critics have criticised for its indifference 'to issues of power, politics and ideology'.[62]

Good economic theory is defined as that which can generate interesting 'if . . . then . . .' propositions that can be tested against reality.[63] But the 'reality' that is preferred by economists consists of readily accessible data sets that are amenable to analysis using sophisticated quantitative techniques. The only conceivable role for a business historian would be to take a checklist of factors that economists are interested in and visit as many archives as possible in the least possible time in order to construct an original data set as a representation of reality.

As far as economists are concerned business historians should refrain from 'the writing of largely unrelated case studies'.[64] They should forego the beguiling 'pleasures of narrative'[65] and avoid any temptation to let 'their varied source material' distract them into historiographical debates that are of no interest to economists in order to address 'a consistent set of questions' posed by economic theory.[66] This amounts to a severe limitation, especially considering the historiographical debates that efficiency theory makes little or no connection with, such as the role of the corporation as a political actor, the perpetuation of race and gender inequalities within the corporation, and the political sustainability of extreme income inequality in a corporate economy.[67]

Arguably rational choice theory, which organizational economics is merely a slightly relaxed version of, is incompatible with narrative history.[68] The ontological assumption that individuals are intuitive economists maximising their utility undercuts a historical view that people's actions are the outcome of a constant internalised dialogue that is influenced by the stories they hear and tell themselves and which can be reconstructed by the historian.

Of course an understanding of economic theory might occasionally provide an insight for narrative company history, just as reading a narrative company history could sometimes suggest an idea for an economic model to an economic theorist. But for the most part they must remain separate activities. Narrative business history provides rich, flesh and blood descriptions of individual businesses, whereas organizational economics is satisfied with a parsimonious, minimalist characterisation, confined to the main characteristics that are necessary and sufficient for actual, historically observable firms to operate. Economic theory offers no more guidance for crafting a narrative historical case study, or criteria for assessing one, than narrative history does for constructing or critiquing an economic model.

Economists are prone to claim that their methodology makes their work scientifically superior to narrative history. Were they to admit otherwise they would 'have to consign [economics] to the status of a *genre*, a stylistic tradition in literature' that is no less susceptible to literary criticism than narrative history.[69] In response to post-modernism, some economists have acknowledged that the metaphorical models used in economics are no less rhetorical than historical narratives, but as yet post-modernism has made little impact on the discourse of organizational economics.

Were business historians to adopt a theoretical framework from organizational economics, narrative case studies would have to be banished from business history to an entirely separate realm of literary company history that economists would deem to be unscientific and therefore devoid of theory. Business history would no longer be 'largely what historians say it is'.[70]

Organizational sociology

Prior to the rise of organizational economics, organization theory was virtually synonymous with organizational sociology, and more specifically with the research program that has become known as structural contingency, which continues to provide the theoretical foundations for leading textbooks in the field.[71] The dominance of structural contingency theory has been challenged by the emergence of rival research programmes, of which two of the most prominent are organizational ecology and new institutionalism, as well as the continuing critique from strategic choice perspectives.[72] I will briefly outline the three research programmes and their treatment of history before rehearsing the strategic choice critique within organizational sociology and its implications for business historians.

Structural contingency

Structural contingency theory, organizational ecology, and new institutionalism can be distinguished from each other most clearly in relation to their competing views of organizational change. Structural contingency and new institutionalism allow for the capacity of organizations to adapt to their environment. In structural contingency theory it is assumed that managers are engaged in an incremental process of autonomous structural adaptation of their organizations in order to maintain the best fit between the structural characteristics of their organization and a changing environment.[73]

Structural contingency displays similar ahistorical tendencies as organizational economics. Its advocates have claimed that processes are too varied to provide a systematic basis for understanding organizations.[74] This argument has been refined into a manifesto:

> The theory and empirical evidence deployed in the structural contingency theory paradigm are positivist. The organization is seen

as being forced to adjust its structure to material factors such as size and technology. Ideas and values do not figure prominently as causes. Moreover, little scope is seen for choice or human volition. There is little information in most contingency analyses about who exactly makes the structural decisions or what their motives are or how the structures are implemented.

The analysis is 'depersonalized', and there is an absence of 'analysis at the level of the human actors'.[75]

The trajectory of structural contingency theory exemplifies the tendency in social science whereby new areas for research are opened up, develop increasingly complex theories and refined measures, and then 'fizzle out in technicism'.[76] This has been exacerbated in organizational sociology by the fear that *'The economists are coming!'* to take over organization theory.[77] Some organizational sociologists have used this fear to argue that sociological research on organizations should be focused around the few paradigms that have generated technologies for replicating research.[78] In these terms, structural contingency counts as one of the most successful paradigms in organizational sociology

The structure priority of structural contingency favors studies that are synchronous and cross-sectional. Extensive research designs with large populations are preferred to longitudinal case studies. It would be difficult, if not impossible, to apply the preferred research instrument retrospectively, since it consists of a highly standardized survey questionnaire administered to a large sample of organizations. A real time longitudinal replication of the survey would be feasible, even if costly and largely pointless, and to the best of my knowledge it has not been attempted. But otherwise anything resembling historical research, let alone narrative history, is more or less precluded from the structural contingency research programme.

Organizational ecology

Adherents of organizational ecology describe it as a 'selection' theory, as opposed to the 'adaptation' theories of structural contingency and new institutionalism, because of its emphasis on structural inertia within organizations. By analogy with Darwinian natural selection of biological organisms, change within populations of organizations is seen as the outcome of four basic processes: variation, selection, retention, and competition. This means that ecological research focuses on the rates of founding and failure of different types of organization as the major source of change in populations of organizations, rather than incremental changes within organizations themselves.[79]

The influence of biology on organizational ecology has meant that its advocates have distanced themselves from the strict determinism found in structural contingency. It is claimed that the 'models and analyses' of organizational ecology are only 'formally probabilistic' rather than 'deterministic'. Organizational ecologists maintain that they do not 'think that the history of organizational populations is preordained to unfold in fixed ways.'[80] But for all the claims that organizational ecology is historical and non-deterministic, it is the one theory of organization in which narrative case studies are explicitly denigrated.

From the ecological 'perspective of explaining variability in the organizational world, the motivations and preferences of particular actors probably do not matter very much.' What is more:

> There is no escaping the antiheroic implications of population ecology. A retrospective analysis of any industry, market, or form of organizing can identify individuals whose actions appear with hindsight to have stood out from their peers. The myths that develop around these people are magnified and romanticized by undisciplined retrospective analysis.

As far as organizational ecology is concerned, 'individual managers do not matter much in accounting for variability in organizational properties'. As for 'the tenacity of explanation at the single-organization level', this probably 'persists partly because it is easier to empathize with single cases than with populations'.[81]

Organizational ecology is noted for its 'use of large-scale, historical databases'.[82] As with economics, the preference is for relatively complete, publicly available data sets. This means that the focus on populations of smaller organizations with a high turnover in ecological research is driven by methodological convenience, analogous to the biologists' use of the fruit fly, rather than a questioning of the economic or cultural significance of large firms that concerns some business historians.[83]

The treatment of time in the longitudinal research programmes in organizational sociology is also problematic from a historical perspective. The time frame is usually only calendar time and presumes a simple account of history. The compression or elongation of events over time is methodologically excluded. Historical time, as opposed to calendrical time, is uneven and punctured by events, but events that rupture the relatively enduring patterns of social life are necessarily excluded from the longitudinal research programmes in organizational sociology. It is almost second nature for historians to identify turning points that 'denote a discontinuity which concatenates into system-wide, unanticipated changes'.[84] For historians, 'Continuity and discontinuity are narrative devices, to be chosen for their storytelling virtues',[85] but in longitudinal ecological studies, as in economics, time is smoothed in an effort to 'trade-off precision and realism for generality'.[86]

New institutionalism

There is scepticism in new institutionalism toward the notions from structural contingency that there is a best fit between an organizational structure and its environment, or that managers engage in autonomous rational action. Instead, organizational change is seen as the outcome of a tendency towards the 'homogeneity of organizational forms and practices' within 'organizational fields'. This tendency has been termed 'isomorphism', which is defined as 'a constraining process that forces one unit in a population to resemble other units that face the same set of environmental conditions'. Three mechanisms are identified through which isomorphic change occurs. These are: coercive isomorphism, which stems from political influence and the need for organizations to secure legitimacy; mimetic isomorphism, which results from the tendency to make standard responses when faced with uncertainty; and normative isomorphism, which is associated with the professionalisation of organizational careers, such that 'individuals who make it to the top are virtually indistinguishable'.[87]

Unlike structural contingency and organizational ecology, new institutionalism does not have a standard research methodology: 'Studies have relied on a variety of techniques, including case analysis, cross-sectional regression, longitudinal models of various types, and so forth'.[88] The methodological flexibility of new institutionalism has facilitated historical research that is notable for its attempt to operationalise competing theories of organizational change, rather than replicate findings using the established research instrument of a single theoretical programme. For example, alternative theories of organizational change have been tested as explanations for the adoption of the multidivisional structure among the hundred largest firms in the USA between 1919 and 1979. Of the five theories tested, support was found for the strategy-structure thesis (Chandler), mimetic isomorphism, and the theory of control based on power. No support was found for organizational ecology or transaction cost economics.[89]

In response to new institutionalism some business historians have acknowledged the 'potential for productive empirical-theoretical exchanges' between business history and organizational sociology.[90] In particular, new institutionalism has given an impetus to historical research into interorganizational relations. It is also seen as supportive of the challenge to the 'simplified, naturalistic, and linear tales of advance and decay' that prevail in business history, reinforced by organizational economics.[91] Nevertheless, new institutionalism, like organizational ecology, has been criticised for its treatment of 'organizations as atoms subject to the law of large numbers and other macropressures that force populations of firms into an equilibrium state.' Organizational ecology and new institutionalism have reoriented organizational sociology from cross-sectional research to 'the more advanced study of a smaller number of variables over long historical time periods'. But they have done so 'at the expense of understanding the uniqueness of individual organizations' from 'richly contextual case studies of single organizations'.[92]

Strategic choice

Unlike organizational economics, the discourse of organizational sociology includes within it a counterweight to the tendencies towards functionalism and determinism. This reflects the 'antinomies' of 'structure' and 'action' that pervade social theory, and which sociologists have highlighted and continually tried to transcend with concepts such as 'structuration'.[93] As an antidote to excessive functionalism in structural contingency theory it has been argued that 'research designed to establish statistically the presence of associations between organizational characteristics usually leaves underlying processes to be inferred.' This approach is deemed to be 'inadequate primarily because it fails to give due attention to the agency of choice by whoever has the power to direct the organization.' The main contention of the strategic choice perspective is that:

> "strategic choice" extends to the context within which the organization is operating, to the standards of performance against which the pressure of economic constraints has to be evaluated, and to the design of the organization's structure itself. Incorporation of the process whereby strategic decisions are made directs attention onto the degree of choice which can be exercised in respect of organizational design, whereas many available models direct attention exclusively onto the constraints involved.[94]

Attempts have been made to absorb many of the objections raised by strategic choice into the structural contingency research programme simply by adding to the list of salient contingencies. In particular, while structural contingency originally sought to discover universal features of organizations that would be found in all national settings, this has been amended to allow for national culture as a significant independent variable.[95] But the use of sophisticated questionnaires to uncover the characteristics of national cultures has subverted rather than complemented the in-depth understandings of national institutions and cultures offered by historians and anthropologists.

In response to the strategic choice critique, defenders of structural contingency theory argue that the 'call for more explanation of organizational structure by reference to elements such as the values, perceptions, ideologies and power of decision-makers' does not escape determinism. Rather it embraces 'sociological determinism', 'since these factors are themselves widely held to be situationally determined'.[96]

In contrast to defenders of structural contingency, advocates of new institutionalism are wary of lapsing into a 'rather mechanical', 'oversocialized conception' of 'how society influences individual behavior' as a reaction against the '*under*socialized conception of human action' in organizational economics.[97] Such a lapse would make historical case studies just as redundant as organizational economics, since neither under-socialised *homo economicus* nor over-socialised *homo sociologicus* have much need of narrative to make sense of their actions. Historians have made the point that sociological determinism allows no role for contingency in history that is comprehended through narrative.[98]

The invocation of history is a refrain in the critiques of theoretical overdetermination and excessive methodological technicism in organizational sociology. The appeal to history for support in the argument for greater attention to the process of organizational change has several implications for the relationship between organizational sociology and business history. In the first place the strategic choice perspective has licensed forays into business archives by organizational sociologists themselves. The best of these have incorporated the tension between action and structure in 'analytically structured narratives'[99] that are self-consciously situated 'on the bridge between narrative and analytic schemas.'[100] In other words they have attempted to strike a balance between the un-theorised commonsense empirical accounts of what actually happened that are often produced by business historians, and the over-theorised accounts produced by sociologists and economists which explain the structural necessity underlying events that have already been recounted by historians.

Rather than attempt to superimpose sociological concepts such as 'structuration' on to historical narratives, the discourse of organizational sociology suggests a way of reading previously published business history to discern the emphasis given to structure and action.[101] For example, Chandler's work on the multidivisional structure has been represented in popular management literature as simplistic determinism,[102] and it has been interpreted as a version of structural contingency theory in organization theory.[103] But these interpretations render redundant the hundreds of pages of detailed historical narrative that Chandler has written. In a detailed reading of Chandler's work, an organizational sociologist points out that in tracing 'how and why the multidivisional structure was invented and adopted' Chandler combines a 'functional argument with individual-level explanations, which is not the same as a simple rational actor model at the individual level'.[104] Chandler not only explains how the environment created problems and opportunities for individual actors, namely the executives of industrial enterprises, he also gives a convincing account of how these executives responded to their environment in ways that were by no means predetermined. The implicit counterfactual argument is that were it not for the organizational innovations of named individuals, companies might not have responded to their environment in the way that they did and the modern economy might consist of an alternative set of institutions.

The diffusion of the multidivisional structure, and other organizational forms, and their effect on performance, lends itself to statistical studies by economists using published sources.[105] But Chandler's work is concerned as much with the process of innovation itself as with the diffusion of organizational forms. Thus it has been argued that 'Chandler's analysis' of the relationship between strategy and structure 'leads to the conclusion that strategic choice is the critical variable in a theory of organizations.'[106] Although Chandler does not acknowledge it, there is a tension in his work between a structural analysis of 'the conditions calling for change' and an action orientation to 'the process of innovation'. According to Chandler himself, 'Only a study of a company's internal business documents and letters can accurately reveal the details of structural reorganization.'[107]

I readily acknowledge that business historians who are familiar with social theory and the philosophy of history, as opposed to the narrow preoccupations of economics, have already produced outstanding narratives that steer a path between voluntarism and determinism without reference to the discourse of organizational sociology.[108] More generally, several best-selling books by historians in recent years have been predicated upon various degrees of ironic and self-conscious rejection of overly structural and deterministic historical writing in favour of more biographical and narrative approaches.[109]

My argument is that the discourse of organizational sociology, unlike organizational economics, need not necessarily relegate historical research to merely providing empirical tests of hypotheses that have been specified in advance. Were business historians to accept the invitation to join in a conversation with organizational sociologists,[110] I hope that they could be enlisted to help separate structural contingency theory, new institutionalism, and organizational ecology from their narrow, technicist, research agendas. Instead they can be used to provide templates of organizational change for incorporation into analytically structured historical narratives and for discerning the emphasis given to different sources of organizational change in previously published company histories. I am not claiming any more for organizational sociology than that it facilitates an increased awareness of the balance between impersonal structural factors and the actions of individuals that can assist in structuring narrative interpretations of company histories. Such an awareness is already implicit in the best, theoretically informed historical writing.

Organizational culture

There is increasing agreement among business historians that 'greater attention to culture can help the practice of business history',[111] and draw it to 'the centre of the study of management'.[112] But I believe that if this is to be achieved there needs to be much greater clarity among business historians concerning the organizational culture discourse. In the first place it has to be acknowledged that the discourse is characterised by acrimony and dissent.[113] But rather than preclude debate by dividing the discourse into mutually exclusive camps, I prefer to follow the argument that it consists of three overlapping levels of analysis.[114] These have been characterised as corporate culturism, organizational symbolism, and post-modernism.[115] I will give a brief outline of each of these, along with an assessment of their implications for historical research.

Corporate culturism

The popular literature on corporate culture rests on an assumption that every organization has a culture of its own, which consists of 'a system of shared meaning held by members that distinguishes the organization from other organizations.'[116] It is this assumption that characterises corporate culturism. The idea that every organization possesses its own unique culture lends itself to historical research and a narrative account of the discrete history of an organization, especially since it is widely accepted that 'organizations begin to create cultures through the actions of founders'.[117]

Notwithstanding the endorsement of the importance of narrative history from corporate culturism, it should be noted that a focus on culture entails a significant reorientation of historical research for business historians. Chandler has expressed a preference for 'institutional' history, as opposed to 'psychological' history, and he has endorsed warnings against 'books on historical myths, symbols, images, and the like'.[118] But from the outset corporate culturism has been associated with a view of entrepreneurs 'not only as creators of some of the more rational and tangible aspects such as structures and technologies but also as creators of symbols, ideologies, languages, beliefs, rituals, and myths'.[119]

The influence of Chandler has led business historians to concentrate on the formal strategies and structures of organizations, which privileges certain kinds of data, such as the board minutes of companies. The evidence for formal organizational structures exists, first and foremost, in the form of official organization charts. But a move towards researching culture calls for alternative types of evidence. Artefacts, such as buildings and works magazines, are obviously manifestations of culture, and the values of a founder may be revealed through personal correspondence, but the basic underlying assumptions are likely to be more elusive.[120]

Corporate culturism provides a welcome justification for the use of oral history,[121] but it also raises a number of problems. Most obviously, if culture is best explored by in-depth, qualitative interviewing, then dead people tell no tales. So cultural research may be restricted to the relatively recent past.[122] More importantly, the nature of interview data reinforces the problem that: 'Real history is fantastically complex, difficult to unravel, and itself culture bound . . . cultures simplify and reinterpret the events to fit into themes that make cultural sense'.[123]

Business historians are inclined to treat interviews as a fact gathering exercise that they can use to check the details and resolve the contradictions from other sources in order to produce a coherent narrative.[124] But a cultural interview needs to be approached as an interaction in which the researcher tries to learn how people see, understand and interpret their past. Recollections of how a culture was created in the past are inevitably filtered through the cultural preoccupations of the present, both on the part of the interviewer as well as the interviewee.

Organizational symbolism

A significant factor in the rise of the organizational culture discourse has been disillusionment with the technicist research programmes in organizational sociology, which 'encourage researchers to separate themselves from the phenomena that make up organizational life and spend limited time – if any – in organizations to collect their data'.[125] Organizational symbolists have favoured 'thick' descriptions of organizations, based on in-depth ethnographic case studies that can take years to complete,[126] as opposed to the 'thin', 'smash and grab' research using a few interviews with senior managers that corporate culturists are often content to rely upon.[127]

The legitimation of in-depth qualitative research and long-term relationships with the members of particular organizations may suggest that organizational symbolism is compatible with business historians' detailed narrative company case studies, but I would like to draw attention to at least two reasons why this is not so. I see these as being, first, the rejection of founder-centred narratives, and second, subjectivism.

One of the only defining characteristics of organizational symbolism is its critique of corporate culturism. A major criticism of corporate culturism is that it is 'founder-centred'. The 'tendency to see the organizational culture as a reflection of the founder's beliefs and values – "the founder writ large"', has been dismissed as 'simplistic and misleading'.[128] It can be seen as a manifestation of the assumption that an organization is possessed of a unitary, and by implication historically continuous culture, rather than discontinuous, cross-cutting, sub-cultures.[129] Much business history can obviously be criticised for being founder-centred, and what business historians have referred to as corporate culture is often no more than the top management culture, with little discussion of whether it is 'accepted or even noticed by lower-level employees'.[130]

A parallel can be drawn between the antipathy of organizational symbolism towards founder-centred corporate culturism, and the hostility of social historians towards the traditional Great Man theory of history. Corporate culturism is a version of the Great Man theory of leadership, in which leaders are portrayed as 'culture creators and culture transformers', whereas organizational symbolists 'generally focus on subcultures rather than an individual leader. Leadership, when it is made visible, is exercised by groups whose members – usually – remain nameless'.[131] The division between corporate culturism and organizational symbolism should not be confused with the dichotomy between the 'breathless accounts of corporate triumph' and 'muckraking tales of managerial corruption' that bothers business historians.[132] Both the hagiographies and the pathographies are versions of the Great Man theory of history.

Business historians have distanced themselves from the 'popular and evangelistic' versions of corporate culturism.[133] But one of the most important differences between corporate culturism and organizational symbolism is that the former is associated with an 'objectivist position' whereas the latter is inclined to a 'subjectivist orientation'.[134] However any move towards subjectivism would tend to undermine the claims by business historians that by being 'scholarly, accurate, fair, objective and serious'[135] they are able to steer a path between 'self serving celebrations' and 'sensational exposés' of a company's history.[136] The elimination rather than admission of bias is a preoccupation of objectivists.[137]

Organizational symbolists maintain that 'detached objectivity in organizational research is largely a myth',[138] and that the subjectivity of the researcher is a particularly significant factor in ethnographic research because it is the product of an active relationship between the researcher, the research community and the actors in the organizational setting that is being researched.[139] But business historians have generally proclaimed their independence and objectivity, especially when they have entered into a relationship with an organization by accepting a commission to write an official company history. From an organizational symbolist perspective such proclamations may be seen as 'evidence of epistemological naivete, methodological sloppiness, or inexcusable political bias'.[140]

Business historians may be right to point out that neither their own nor their corporate sponsor's reputations would be enhanced if they were to produce a 'whitewash', and it seems only reasonable to take their word for it that in most cases corporate sponsors have not censored their work.[141] But there is no need to question a historian's integrity in order to suggest that the process of commissioning favours a particular kind of historian writing a distinctive form of history. For example, it seems reasonable to suppose that companies are more likely to commission their histories to be written, and subsequently to publish them, when they are sufficiently confident of their reputation in the present to be able to withstand any revelations about their past. The very fact that an organization has been in existence long enough to consider commissioning its own history makes for a teleological narrative of success, as if the organization was possessed of the secret recipe for longevity.

Post-modernism

The parallel between organizational symbolism and social history can be extended, inasmuch as the rise of organizational symbolism can be seen as corresponding to the 'linguistic turn' in social history. Both organizational symbolism and the linguistic turn have been influenced by anthropology,[142] and both have raised many of the issues that have come to be associated with post-modernism. In the organizational culture discourse post-modernism has exacerbated the doubts of organizational symbolism concerning 'prevailing assumptions about the rationality of conducting research and using language in expressing it'.[143]

The organizational symbolists' objection to founder-centred corporate culturism extends to a virtual denial that it is possible to reconstruct a narrative history of an organization in order to identify the source of its culture.[144] Organizational symbolists could be said to share what historians have described as the 'impositionalist' objection to narrative history, which is 'that recounting the past in the form of a story inevitably imposes a false narrative structure upon it'. Historians have construed the impositionalist objection to historical narrative as a license to abandon the commitment to verisimilitude through verification that differentiates history from fiction.[145]

Unfortunately business historians are not well placed to counter the impositionalist objection to historical narratives from post-modernism. Business historians have reacted to post-modernism with a mixture of indifference and complacency.[146] Business history has not been *hit* by post-modernism in the same way that social history obviously has been.[147] There is no sense that business history is in crisis in the same way that the discipline of history itself is said to be.[148] Even if they realise that it is a fallacy to seek total objectivity in history, most business historians probably still see themselves as 'neutralists', in the sense that they try to avoid making overt moral judgements about the past.[149] They remain committed to 'telling the story as it really was', without recognising 'telling the story as it happened' evades the responsibility of 'declaring a point of view'.[150]

It is clear from the 'realist' ripostes to post-modernism from historians and organization theorists that historical narratives can only be defended effectively against the impositionalist objection if it is acknowledged that narratives are theory laden. Thus the charge that business historians are atheoretical empiricists becomes untenable, since it rests on 'an unacknowledged supposition that theory-neutral research is even possible'.[151] Postmodernists in history have called for historians to become more 'reflexive' in dealing with issues of theory, that is, to develop their own self-consciously held position on history and to be in control of their own discourse.[152] Similarly in the organizational culture discourse it is argued that research into organizational culture entails an ongoing engagement with the meaning of the term.[153] If this is accepted then it undermines the claim that business historians 'have been conducting cultural analyses without realising it'.[154]

Business history is only atheoretical to the extent that its conceptualisations and claims are relatively unexamined. Thus it cannot be said that narrative historical accounts of companies are atheoretical just because they lack ostentatiously theoretical language. What they lack is any acknowledgement of the theoretical basis for their interpretation of history. This verges on an assumption that theirs is the commonsense interpretation. But to paraphrase a post-modernist, 'anyone who only knows one interpretation of a company's history does not know any interpretation of it at all',[155] and that applies to most company historians and their readers.

Business historians have attempted to distance themselves from 'the writing of company histories . . . as a form of journalistic hackwork',[156] as if objectivity in itself makes a company history worthy of a reader's attention.[157] But the problem with the pre-modern, self-contained narratives of the sort that are often produced when long-serving employees or antiquarian business historians are commissioned to write the history of a company is not that they lack objectivity, but that they fail to generate or to address controversy.

The post-modernist argument 'that there might be a "fictional" element in the historian's text, however much he or she has tried to avoid it', may appear to many historians, business historians included, to be a 'menace to serious historical study'.[158] Business historians might be expected to line up against post-modernism with the self-proclaimed 'professional' historians, who reckon that the practise of history is about 'not getting it wrong'.[159] However, the stream of post-modernism in historical writing that 'is informed by a programmatic, if ironic, commitment to the return to narrative as one of its enabling presuppositions',[160] has been credited with reinstating 'good writing as legitimate historical practice'.[161] This is in stark contrast to the version of post-modernism encountered in the organizational culture discourse, which is more likely to 'finish off any author, and any reader', with 'its ambiguities and slipperiness'.[162] All of this suggests that there is scope for historians to intervene in the organizational culture discourse in order to counter the corrosive effects of post-modernism.

Conclusion

One of the reasons that business historians are seeking a more theoretical orientation is that they are under increasing pressure to find a home in business schools. Some of them seem to believe that they can by-pass the need for any theoretical engagement with other business school faculty by demonstrating the pedagogical value of business history for business students.[163] They take heart from the reported popularity of business history electives among Harvard MBA students.[164] But it must be obvious that the status of business history at Harvard Business School rests upon the research reputations of Harvard business historians in general, and in particular the influence of 'Chandlerism' in the study of corporate strategy and organization theory. Which suggests that, like it or not, business historians will have to demonstrate the relevance of historical research in relation to the theoretical concerns of other well-established fields of business school research in order to establish their credibility in research oriented business schools. Those business historians who are unwilling to engage with other researchers in business schools may find that they are resented by the anthropologists, economists, sociologists and psychologists, amongst others, who have had to adapt when moving into business schools from their home disciplines.[165]

Rather than ignore theoretical developments in the social sciences and humanities, I propose that by entering into a dialogue with organization theory business historians would be better able to indicate their preferences for the theoretical orientations of different disciplines. My own preferences should be fairly clear by now. Business historians may be inclined towards an affinity with organizational economics, ambivalence towards organizational sociology, and indifference or even antipathy towards the form of post-modernism that is favoured in the organizational culture discourse. But I maintain that organizational economics threatens to undermine the legitimacy of narrative company case studies more than organizational sociology, while a considered response to post-modernism might even rejuvenate narrative historical writing.

If business history is defined as 'the systematic study of individual firms on the basis of their business records',[166] then organizational economics appears to have little to offer. In my view, Chandler's advice that, 'A historian's task is not merely to borrow other people's theories or even to test their theories for them',[167] stands as a warning against subordinating business history to economic theories of organization. The lack of an audience for much narrative company history can be attributed to it having addressed too few historiographical debates, rather than too many, as alleged by economists. The abstention from historiographical debate results from the implicit belief of business historians that by concentrating on 'setting the record straight' they can avoid contentious disputes. Were business historians to consciously eschew economic models then their case studies could be used explicitly to address a range of historiographical debates that would be of potential interest to a much broader readership than the cognoscente of economic theory.[168]

Business historians may feel obliged to defer to economists on the grounds that business is self evidently an economic phenomenon and because business history developed as a branch of economic history. But it is clear from organization theory that economics came late to the theorisation of economic organization,[169] by which time organizational sociology was already well established. What is more, the advance of economic imperialists into subject areas such as sex and politics has undermined the notion that sociology and economics are discrete disciplines that are concerned with separate social and economic phenomena respectively. If economics and sociology can be defined as anything more than genres of writing, then it is by their methodologies rather than their subject matter.

Organizational sociologists have argued that 'the chosen approach' to a subject 'is not a function of what is being studied but *represents the preferences of the researcher for how research should be done*'.[170] Or as post-modernists have put it: 'Content is a derivative of style'.[171] If business historians prefer the theoretical orientation of organizational economics, then it might be appreciated if they could deign indicate the basis for their preference, especially in relation to the criticisms directed against organizational economics from other discourses in organization theory. The frequent assertion that this or that economic theory is useful for business historians carries with it an implicit argument that other theories are less useful, but business historians rarely make explicit their criteria for assessing the usefulness of alternative theories.

Business historians seem to take it as given that business history 'should evolve from producing well-written empirical historical case studies to delivering valid generalisations about business structures and behaviour'.[172] But theory development in economics is deductive and does not proceed from the accumulation of empirical case studies, while in organizational sociology the relationship between historical description and theoretical development remains problematic.[173] Insofar organizational sociology is dominated by technicist research programmes, such as those of structural contingency and organizational ecology, which are driven by deterministic and probabilistic theories respectively, it leaves little scope for an account of the contingent events and the volition of actors that are captured by narrative historical case studies. But the discourse of organizational sociology does highlight the possibilities of making historical case studies explicitly theoretical in themselves, and of analysing the theory embedded in case studies that are not explicitly theoretical, in terms of the balance between structure and action, or determinism and voluntarism. By insisting on the need for narrative case studies to be accommodated by theories of organization I feel that business historians can contribute to the reconceptualization of organization theory as a 'humanistic enterprise' as well as a 'scientific enterprise'.[174]

Business historians complain that the potential of company histories 'to inform contemporary managerial decision-making, influence public opinion, and enhance scientific knowledge of firms – seems to remain unrealized'.[175] But they are reluctant to reflect on what it is about the conventions that define the genre of scholarly company histories which ensures that most of them remain unread, even by other academic business historians. I contend that such reflection would be facilitated if business historians were to participate in the discourse of organizational culture. Countering the impositionalist objections to historical narratives from organizational symbolists would help business historians to make a connection with the theoretical developments around post-modernism that have taken place in the discipline of history itself, which hitherto they have ignored.[176]

Business history is often presented as an endeavour to 'fill in the gaps' in knowledge,[177] as if a history of Snooks & Co should be welcomed as a contribution to the grand data collection exercise in which one day the history of every company that ever existed will have been written. Business historians are so obsessed with ensuring that the facts presented in the history of Snooks & Co are *true* facts that they have lost sight of any notion that they should be *interesting* facts, which will contribute to historiographical debates and generate further research and writing.[178] Sadly it can be said that all too many business historians have succeeded in having the last word on the history of a company. My hope is that by engaging with theory, whether from the discourses of organization theory or from elsewhere, business historians will be able to establish the cultural significance, rather than the technical usefulness, of the competing narratives of company histories.

Notes

1 Recent conferences of business historians have addressed issues of history and theory. See P. Scranton and R. Horowitz 1997, '"The future for business history" An introduction', *Business and Economic History*, 26: 2 (1997) pp. 1–4; T. Slaven (ed.), *Business History, Theory and Practice* (Centre for Business History in Scotland, 2000).

2 L. Hannah, 'Entrepreneurs and the social sciences', *Economica*, 51 (1984), p. 219.

3 M. Rowlinson, 'The early application of Scientific Management by Cadbury', *Business History* 30 (1988), pp. 377–395; M. Rowlinson, *Organisations and Institutions: Perspectives in Economics and Sociology* (London: Macmillan, 1997).

4 P. Clark, *Organisations in Action* (London: Routledge, 2000), p. 37.

5 J. Hassard, *Sociology and Organization Theory* (Cambridge University Press, 1993).

6 O. E. Williamson, 'Chester Barnard and the incipient science of organization theory', in O. E. Williamson (ed.), *Organization Theory* (Oxford: Oxford University Press, 1995), pp. 172–206.

7 M. Rowlinson and S. Procter, 'Organizational culture and business history', *Organization Studies*, 20 (1999), pp. 369–396; A. Kieser, 'Why organization theory needs historical analyses – And how these should be performed', *Organization Science*, 5 (1994), pp. 608–620.

8 For an overview of organization theory see S. R. Clegg and C. Hardy (eds), *Studying Organization: Theory & Method* (London: Sage, 1999).

9 J. B. Barney and W. Hesterly, 'Organizational economics: Understanding the relationship between organizations and economic analysis', in Clegg and Hardy, *Studying Organization*.

10 L. Donaldson, 'The normal science of structural contingency theory'; J. A. C. Baum, 'Organizational ecology'; P. S. Tolbert and L. G. Zucker, 'The institionalization of institutional theory', all in Clegg and Hardy, *Studying Organization*.

11 J. Martin and P. Frost, 'The organizational culture war games: A struggle for intellectual dominance', in Clegg and Hardy, *Studying Organization*.

12 Hannah, 'Entrepreneurs', p. 223; D. C. Coleman, 'The uses and abuses of business history', *Business History*, 29 (1987), p. 151.

13 E. Penrose, *The Theory of the Growth of the Firm* (Oxford: Basil Blackwell, 1959), p. 13; Rowlinson, *Organisations and Institutions*, p. 13.

14 E.g. A. Alchian, 'Uncertainty, evolution, and economic theory', *Journal of Political Economy*, LVIII (1950), p. 211–21. For critiques see L. Hannah, Introduction to *Management Strategy and Business Development: An Historical and Comparative Study* (Macmillan, 1976), p. 6; Hannah 'Entrepreneurs', p. 220.

15 N. R. Lamoreaux, D. M. G. Raff and P. Temin, 'New economic approaches to the study of business history', *Business and Economic History*, 26: 1 (1997), pp. 57–79. See also M. Casson and M. B. Rose, 'Institutions and the evolution of modern business: Introduction', *Business History*, XXXIX (1997), pp. 1–8.

16 J. F. Wilson, *British Business History, 1720–1994* (Manchester: Manchester University Press, 1995), pp. 16–17; R. H. Coase, *The Firm, the Market and the Law* (London: University of Chicago Press, 1990); Penrose, *Theory of the Growth*.

17 Barney and Hesterly, 'Organizational Economics', p. 128.

18 S. Estape-Triay, 'Business history and institutional economic theory', in Slaven, *Business History*, p. 20.

19 H. Scarbrough, 'Path(ological) dependency? Core competencies from an organizational perspective', *British Journal of Management*, 9 (1998), p. 228.

20 O. E. Williamson, *The Mechanisms of Governance* (Oxford: Oxford University Press, 1996), p. 240. Williamson is the most prominent exponent of transaction costs in organization theory.

21 O. E. Williamson, 'The modern corporation as an efficiency instrument: The contracting perspective', in C. Kaysen (ed.), *The American Corporation Today* (Oxford: Oxford University Press, 1996).

22 O. E. Williamson, *The Economic Institutions of Capitalism* (London: Free Press, 1985), p. 325.

23 O. E. Williamson, *Markets and Hierarchies* (London: Free Press, 1983), p. 171.

24 H. Demsetz, *Ownership, Control and The Firm*, Volume 1 (Oxford: Basil Blackwell, 1988), p. 23.

25 See M. Granovetter, 'Economic action and social structure: The problem of embeddedness', in M. Granovetter and R. Swedberg (eds), *The Sociology of Economic Life* (Oxford: Westview Press, 1992).

26 Coase, *The Firm*, p. 15.

27 R. Swedberg and M. Granovetter, Introduction to *The Sociology of Economic Life*, p. 15.

28 S. R. H. Jones, 'Transaction costs and the theory of the firm', *Business History*, 39 (1997), p. 15.

29 M. Neimark and T. Tinker, 'Identity and non-identity thinking: A dialectical critique of the transaction cost theory of the modern corporation', *Journal of Management*, 13 (1987), p. 668n.

30 P. Marginson, 'Power and efficiency in the firm: Understanding the employment relationship', in C. Pitelis (ed.), *Transaction Costs, Markets, and Hierarchies* (Oxford: Basil Blackwell, 1993), p. 149.

31 Jones, 'Transaction costs', p. 19.

32 P. M. Hirsch and M. D. Lounsbury, 'Rediscovering volition: The institutional economics of Douglass C. North', *Academy of Management Review*, 21 (1996), pp. 872–884; D. C. North, *Institutions, Institutional Change and Economic Performance* (Cambridge University Press, 1990), p. 9.

33 J. Lott, 'In celebration of Armen Alchian's 80th birthday: Living and breathing economics', *Economic Inquiry*, July (1996), pp. 412–3.

34 G. M. Hodgson, *Economics and Institutions: A Manifesto for Modern Institutional Economics* (Cambridge: Polity, 1988), p. 214; D. N. McCloskey, *The Rhetoric of Economics* (Brighton: Wheatsheaf, 1986), p. 15.

35 R. F. Freeland, 'The myth of the M-Form? Governance, consent, and organizational change', *American Journal of Sociology*, 102 (1996), p. 484n.

36 Granovetter, 'Economic action', p. 72.

37 T. Kuran, 'The tenacious past: Theories of personal and collective conservatism', *Journal of Economic Behavior and Organization*, 10 (1988), p. 144.

38 S. Bowles and H. Gintis, 'Power in competitive exchange' in S. Bowles, M. Franzini & U. Pagano (eds), *The Politics and Economics of Power* (London: Routledge, 1999).

39 D. N. McCloskey, *Knowledge and Persuasion in Economics* (Cambridge University Press: 1994), p. 156.

40 E.g. Barney and Hesterly, 'Organizational Economics'.

41 Casson and Rose, 'Institutions', p. 4.

42 Barney and Hesterly, 'Organizational Economics', p. 136.
43 M. Zey, *Rational Choice Theory and Organizational Theory: A Critique* (London: Sage, 1998).
44 Williamson, *Mechanisms of Governance*, p. 240.
45 Lamoreaux, Raff and Temin, 'New economic approaches', p. 77.
46 G. J. Stigler, 'Economics – The imperial science?' *Scandinavian Journal of Economics*, 86 (1984), pp. 301–13.
47 J. Hirschleifer, 'Economics from a biological point of view', *Journal of Law and Economics*, 20 (1977), pp. 3–4.
48 P. J. Buckley and M. Casson, 'Economics as an imperialist social science', *Human Relations*, 46 (1993), pp. 1035–52.
49 J. B. Barney and W. G. Ouchi, 'Learning from organizational economics', in J. B. Barney and W. G. Ouci (eds), *Organizational Economics* (Jossey-Bass, 1986), p. 423.
50 M. Casson, 'Culture as an economic asset', in A. Godley and O. M. Westall (eds), *Business History and Business Culture* (Manchester University Press, 1996), p. 49.
51 P. Ghemawat, Book Review, *Journal of Economic Literature*, XXXVIII (2000), pp. 419–20.
52 R. Posner, *Sex and Reason* (London: Harvard UP, 1992), p. 89.
53 D. Wittman 'Political parties, pressure groups, and democracy: A transaction cost theory of political institutions', in Bowles, Franzini and Pagano, *Politics and Economics*.
54 Clark, *Organisations*, p. 90.
55 D. N. McCloskey, *If You're So Smart: The Narrative of Economic Expertise* (Chicago: University of Chicago Press, 1990), p. 22.
56 Casson, 'Culture as an economic asset', p. 49.
57 Lamoreaux, Raff and Temin, 'New economic approaches', p. 77.
58 M. Shanley, 'Straw men and M-Form myths: Comment on Freeland', *American Journal of Sociology*, 102 (1996), p. 533.
59 Barney and Hesterly, 'Organizational Economics', p. 114.
60 M. Ricketts, *The Economics of Business Enterprise: New Approaches to the Firm* (London: Harvester Wheatsheaf, 1987), p. 266.
61 P. Scranton, *Endless Novelty: Specialty Production and American Industrialization, 1865–1925* (Princeton University Press, 1997), p. 7.
62 R. B. DuBoff and E. S. Herman, 'Alfred Chandler's new business history: A review', *Politics and Society*, 10:1 (1980), pp. 87–110.
63 G. A. Akerlof, *An Economic Theorist's Book of Tales: Essays that Entertain the Consequences of New Assumptions in Economic Theory* (Cambridge University Press, 1984), pp. 2–3.
64 Lamoreaux, Raff and Temin, 'New economic approaches', p. 61.
65 D. C. Coleman, *History and The Economic Past: An Account of the Rise and Decline of Economic History* (Oxford: Clarendon, 1987), p. 145.
66 Coleman, 'uses and abuses', p. 149.
67 Kaysen, 'Introduction and Overview', *The American Corporation*.
68 N. Ferguson 'Introduction, Virtual History: Towards a 'chaotic' theory of the past' in N. Ferguson (ed.), *Virtual History* (London: Papermac, 1997), p. 63.
69 McCloskey, *Knowledge and Persuasion*, p. 250.

70 G. D. Smith and D. Dyer, 'The rise and transformation of the American Corporation', in Kaysen, *The American Corporation*, p. 32.

71 R. Daft, *Organization Theory and Design* (Cincinnati, OH: International Thomson, 1998), p. 25.

72 Other research programmes that could be mentioned include resource dependence and network analysis.

73 L. Donaldson, *For Positivist Organization Theory* (London: Sage, 1996), pp. 170–1.

74 D. S. Pugh and D. J. Hickson, *Aston Programme*, Vol. 1 (London: Saxon House, 1976), p. 1.

75 Donaldson, 'The normal science of structural contingency theory', pp. 57–58.

76 M. N. Zald, 'Organization studies as a scientific and humanistic enterprise: Toward a reconceptualization of the foundations of the field', *Organization Science*, 4:4 (1993), p. 514.

77 J. Van Maanen, 'Fear and loathing in organization studies', *Organization Science*, 6:6 (1995), p. 689.

78 J. Pfeffer, 'Mortality, reproducibility, and the persistence of styles of theory', *Organization Science*, 6:6 (1995), pp. 681–686.

79 Baum, 'Organizational ecology'.

80 M. T. Hannan and J. Freeman, *Organizational Ecology* (Cambridge MA: Harvard University Press, 1989), p. 40.

81 Hannan and Freeman, *Organizational Ecology*, pp. 40–3.

82 Baum, 'Organizational ecology', p. 101.

83 Scranton, *Endless Novelty*.

84 P. Scranton, 'Periodization in 20th century business history: An American perspective', *Turning Points in Business History*, Association of Business Historians Conference Programme, South Bank University, 1999, p. 7.

85 McCloskey, *If You're So Smart*, p. 22.

86 Baum, 'Organizational ecology', p. 101.

87 P. J. DiMaggio and W. W. Powell, 'The iron cage revisited: Institutional isomorphism and collective rationality in organizational fields', in W. W. Powell and P. J. DiMaggio (eds), *The New Institutionalism in Organizational Analysis* (London: University of Chicago Press, 1991).

88 Tolbert and Zucker, 'The institutionalization of institutional theory', p. 169.

89 N. Fligstein 'The spread of the multidivisional form among large firms, 1919–1979', *American Sociological Review*, 50 (1985), pp. 377–91.

90 P. Scranton, 'Webs of productive association in American industrialization: Patterns of institution-formation and their limits, Philadelphia, 1880–1930', *Journal of Industrial History*, 1 (1998), p. 19.

91 Scranton, 'Webs', pp. 18, 26.

92 P. M. Hirsch and M. Lounsbury, 'Putting the organization back into organization theory: Action, change, and the "new" institutionalism', *Organization Science*, 6:1 (1997), p. 80.

93 A. Giddens, *Central Problems in Social Theory* (London: Macmillan, 1979), p. 49; A. Giddens, *The Constitution of Society: Outline of the Theory of Structuration* (Cambridge: Polity, 1986).

94 J. Child, 'Organizational structure, environment and performance: The role of strategic choice', *Sociology*, 6 (1972), pp. 1–2.

95 For a discussion and critique of this trend see Clark, *Organisations*, ch. 8.

96 Donaldson, *For Positivist Organization Theory*, p. 18.
97 Granovetter, 'Economic action', p. 57.
98 Ferguson, 'Virtual history'.
99 Clark, *Organisations*, p. 113.
100 R. Whipp and P. Clark, *Innovation and the Auto Industry: Product, Process and Work Organization* (London: Francis Pinter, 1986), p. 18.
101 J. Yates, 'Using Giddens' structuration theory to inform business history', *Business and Economic History*, 26:1 (1997), pp. 159–183.
102 T. J. Peters and R. H. Waterman, *In Search of Excellence* (New York: Harper & Row, 1982), p. 4.
103 Donaldson, *For Positivist Organization Theory*.
104 A. L. Stinchcombe, *Information and Organizations* (Oxford: University of California Press, 1990), p. 109.
105 E.g. R. P. Rumelt, *Strategy, Structure and Economic Performance* (Cambridge MA: Harvard UP, 1974).
106 Child, 'Organizational structure', p. 15.
107 A. D. Chandler, *Strategy and Structure: Chapters in the History of the Industrial Enterprise* (London: MIT Press, 1962), pp. 299, 380.
108 E.g. N. Ferguson, *The World's Banker: The History of the House of Rothschild* (London: Weidenfield & Nicolson, 1998). For a sociological review of Ferguson see M. Rowlinson, *Human Relations*, 53:4 (2000), pp. 573–586.
109 E.g. S. Schama, *Citizens: A Chronicle of the French Revolution* (London: Penguin, 1989), pp. xv – vi; O. Figes, *A People's Tragedy* (London: Pimlico, 1997), pp. xvii – xix, 455–6; I. Kershaw, *Hitler, 1889–1936: Hubris* (London: Penguin, 1998), p. xii.
110 Zald, 'Organization studies', p. 519.
111 K. Lipartito, 'Culture and the practice of business history', *Business and Economic History*, 24:2 (1995), p. 5.
112 O. M. Westall, 'British business history and the culture of business', in Godley & Westall, *Business History and Business Culture*, p. 21.
113 Martin and Frost, 'The organizational culture war games'.
114 M. Alvesson and P. O. Berg, *Corporate Culture and Organizational Symbolism* (Berlin: Walter de Gruyter, 1992), pp. 2, 200–1.
115 P. Jeffcut, 'From interpretation to representation in organizational analysis: Post-modernism, ethnography and organizational symbolism', *Organization Studies*, 15:2 (1994), pp. 241–274. An alternative terminology refers to 'integration', 'differentiation', and 'fragmentation' perspectives, see J. Martin, *Cultures in Organizations: Three Perspectives* (Oxford University Press, 1992).
116 This definition is taken from one of the leading textbooks, S. P. Robbins, *Organizational Behavior* (Upper Saddle River, New Jersey: Prentice Hall, 8th edn, 1998), p. 595; see also Martin, *Cultures in Organizations*, p. 54.
117 E. H. Schein, *Organizational Culture and Leadership* (San Francisco: Jossey-Bass, 1985), p. 221; Peters and Waterman, *In Search of Excellence*; T. E. Deal and A. A. Kennedy, *Corporate Cultures* (Reading, MA: Addison-Wesley, 1982).
118 A. D. Chandler, *The Essential Alfred Chandler* T. K. McCraw (ed.) (Boston MA: Harvard Business School Press, 1988), p. 302.

119   A. M. Pettigrew, 'On studying organizational cultures', *Administrative Science Quarterly*, 24 (1979), pp. 570–581.

120   Schein, *Organizational Culture*, pp. 14–21; G. Jones, 'Company history and business history in the 1990s', *European Yearbook of Business History*, 2 (1999), pp. 1–20.

121   Jones, 'Company history and business history'.

122   S. Kendrick, P. Straw and D. McCrone (eds), 'Introduction: Sociology and history, the past and the present', *Interpreting the Past, Understanding the Present* (London: Macmillan, 1990), p. 3.

123   Schein, *Organizational Culture*, p. 303.

124   A. Wilkinson, 'Text, lies and a lot of red tape', *Financial Times*, 27 March 1998.

125   H. M. Trice and J. M. Beyer, *The Cultures of Work Organizations* (Englewood Cliffs, NJ: Prentice Hall, 1993), p. 31; Alveson and Berg, *Corporate Culture*, p. 22.

126   Two of the best examples are T. J. Watson, *In Search of Management* (London: International Thomson, 1994); and Martin, *Cultures in Organizations*.

127   Alvesson and Berg, *Corporate Culture*, p. 22; Martin and Frost, 'The organizational culture war games', p. 352.

128   Alvesson and Berg, *Corporate Culture*, p. 61; M. Alvesson, *Cultural Perspectives in Organizations* (Cambridge University Press, 1993), pp. 81–7.

129   M. J. Hatch, *Organization Theory* (Oxford University Press, 1997), p. 226.

130   Martin and Frost, 'The organizational culture war games', p. 350.

131   Martin, *Cultures in Organizations*, pp. 45, 104; J. Martin, S. B. Sitkin and M. Boehm, 'Founders and the elusiveness of a cultural legacy', in P. J. Frost, L. F. Moore, M. R. Louis, C. C. Lundberg and J. Martin (eds), *Organizational Culture* (London: Sage, 1985), p. 100.

132   D. B. Sicilia, 'Remembering Robert Sobel (1931–1999)', *Enterprise and Society* 1:1 (2000), p. 183.

133   A. Godley and O. M. Westall, 'Business history and business culture: An introduction', in Godley and Westall, *Business History and Business Culture*, p. 2.

134   Martin, *Cultures in Organizations*, p. 65.

135   Coleman, 'uses and abuses', p. 142.

136   G. D. Smith and L. E. Steadman, 'Present value of corporate history', *Harvard Business Review*, 59: November–December (1981), p. 164.

137   Martin, *Cultures in Organizations*, p. 66.

138   J. S. Ott, *The Organizational Culture Perspective* (Pacific Grove CA: Brooks/Cole, 1989), p. 101.

139   B. A. Turner, 'Connoisseurship in the study of organizational cultures', in A. Bryman (ed.), *Doing Research in Organizations* (London: Routledge, 1988), p. 114.

140   Martin, *Cultures in Organizations*, p. 11.

141   Ferguson, *The World's Banker*, p. xxi; N. Ferguson, 'He who sups with the devil must use a long spoon – and bring a good agent', *Times Higher Education Supplement*, 25 December 1998.

142   E.g. C. Geertz, *The Interpretation of Cultures* (London: Fontana, 1993).

143   Alvesson and Berg, *Corporate Culture*, pp. 200–1.

144   Martin, Sitkin and Boehm, 'Founders', p. 103.

145 A. P. Norman, 'Telling it like it was: Historical narratives on their own terms', in B. Fay, P. Pomper and R. T. Vann (eds), *History and Theory: Contemporary Readings* (Oxford: Blackwell, 1998), p. 156.

146 E.g. Lipartito, 'Culture and the practice of business history', p. 7; Godley and Westall, 'Business history and business culture', p. 3.

147 Ferguson, *Virtual History*, p. 65; P. Joyce, 'The end of social history?' in K. Jenkins (ed.), *The Postmodern History Reader* (London: Routledge, 1997).

148 R. J. Evans, *In Defence of History* (London: Granta, 1997), p. 4.

149 Coleman, *History and the Economic Past*, pp. 64, 145.

150 McCloskey, *If You're So Smart*, p. 32.

151 A. Sayer, *Realism and Social Science* (London: Sage, 2000), p. 146.

152 K. Jenkins, *Re-Thinking History* (1991).

153 Alvesson, *Cultural Perspectives*, p. 120.

154 O. M. Westall, 'British business history and the culture of business', p. 43.

155 F. R. Ankersmit, 'Historiography and postmodernism', in Fay, Pomper and Vann, *History and Theory*.

156 Coleman, 'Uses and abuses', p. 145.

157 Jones, 'Company history'.

158 H. White, 'Response to Marwick', *Journal of Contemporary History*, 30 (1995), pp. 233–246.

159 A. Marwick, 'Two approaches to historical study: The metaphysical (including post-modernism) and the historical', *Journal of Contemporary History*, 30 (1995), pp. 5–35.

160 H. White, *The Content of the Form: Narrative Discourse and Historical Representation* (Baltimore: Johns Hopkins University Press, 1987), p. xi.

161 Evans, *In Defence of History*, p. 244.

162 M. Alvesson, 'The meaning and meaninglessness of postmodernism', *Organizaton Studies*, 16:6 (1995), pp. 1071.

163 D. Jeremy, 'Do managers need business history?' Business History Workshop, British Academy of Management Conference, Manchester Metropolitan University, 1999. A. Kransdorff, 'The rear-view mirror idea that can transform British industry', *Business History News*, March (2000), pp. 4–8.

164 T. K. McCraw, 'Teaching history courses to Harvard MBA students: Building enrolment from 21 to 1,300', *Business and Economic History*, 28:2 (1999), pp. 153–162.

165 The longstanding tensions in business schools are discussed in H. Simon, 'The business school' in *Administrative Behavior* (New York: Free Press, 3rd edn, 1976).

166 J. Tosh, *The Pursuit of History* (Harlow: Longman, 2nd edn, 1991), p. 95.

167 Chandler, *Essential Alfred Chandler*, pp. 304–5.

168 As Ferguson has done. Ferguson, *The World's Banker*, pp. 31–2.

169 T. A. Marschak, 'Economic theories of organization', in J. G. March (ed.), *Handbook of Organization* (Chicago: Rand McNally, 1965).

170 P. Carter and N. Jackson, 'Qualitative approaches in organisation studies', University of Hull, School of Management Working Paper (1997), p. 5, emphasis in original.

171 Ankersmit, 'Historiography and postmodernism'.

172 Jones, 'Company history'.

173 Zald, 'Organization studies', p. 520.

174 Zald, 'Organization studies'.
175 Jones, 'Company history'.
176 A. Roberts, 'The very idea of theory in business history', University of Reading, Dept of Economics Discussion Paper (1998).
177 Evans, *In Defence of History*, p. 21.
178 Ankersmit, 'Historiography and postmodernism'.

Chapter 2

Management strategies for health

J. W. Roberts and the Armley Asbestos Tragedy, 1920–1958

Geoffrey Tweedale

Introduction

This article presents a case-study in a much neglected area in British industrial history – occupational health and safety. Generally, business historians have much preferred to concentrate on the dynamics of leadership and management rather than the health and safety of the workforce. Consequently in most books, workers' injuries and deaths, if they feature at all, are seen as a side-issue – an unintended result of industrialisation – which only have a marginal impact on business decisions.[1]

To be sure, historians rarely have access to archive material in the 'dangerous trades.' However, in asbestos manufacture we have been lucky. In the last decade, property-damage litigation in America has forced the leading British asbestos producer, Turner & Newall, to disgorge its huge archive into the public domain.[2] Using these records, this article scrutinises the management strategies of J. W. Roberts, an asbestos company in Leeds that was a Turner & Newall subsidiary. Roberts' commercial history is described briefly, but the major focus is on the company's occupational health policies. It attempts to answer a number of key questions: what was the attitude of the Roberts' and Turner & Newall directors to the asbestos health hazard in its factories?; to what extent did the company implement government health regulations?; and how much compensation did the company pay? The role of the Factory Inspectorate and the attitudes of the workers are also examined. Finally, the implications of the Roberts' story for wider perspectives on company strategy and government regulation are discussed.

Commercial background

The Roberts' business was originally located at Moorside, in Armley, a suburb of Leeds. It began in 1874 when John W. Roberts (1856–94) began the manufacture of 'special lubricative engine packings' from hemp, jute or cotton.[3] In the year after his death, the company – which by then had moved to the Midland Works in nearby Canal Road – was converted into a private limited company with a paid up capital of £500. The workforce was tiny (under a dozen), as were profits and turnover. By the turn of the century, the 'magic mineral' asbestos was being used by Roberts. The fireproofing and insulation properties of asbestos gave an immediate boost to the business and the product line expanded to include asbestos cloth and rope, and insulating mattresses for steam boilers in ships and locomotives. In carding and spinning the company used chrysotile ('white' asbestos), but the main raw material was crocidolite ('blue' asbestos) because of its wet strength and superior acid-resisting qualities which were crucial in the mattress trade.

By the end of the First World War, the UK asbestos industry had expanded dramatically, with the leading companies spanning a wide range of activities. These included the overseas mining of asbestos; spinning and weaving asbestos textiles; the manufacture of asbestos cement for roofs and buildings; the production and application of insulation materials; and the development of asbestos brake-linings. In 1920, Turner Brothers Asbestos (TBA) – a Rochdale company with roots in the Lancashire textile trade – organised a merger of the leading firms to form Turner & Newall. The new company included TBA (which also controlled Turner's Asbestos Cement at Trafford Park and various overseas operations); Washington Chemical Co in County Wear (and its contract insulating arm, Newalls); and J. W. Roberts, which was purchased for £100,000. Ferodo, the Derbyshire friction materials manufacturer, was added to the group in 1925. Thereafter Roberts' history was inextricably linked with the development of Turner & Newall, which as the 'Asbestos Giant' rapidly became the leading asbestos company in the UK.[4]

TBA's and Roberts' activities were complementary, with the Rochdale company specialising mainly in chrysotile and Roberts in crocidolite. After rationalisation in the 1920s, Roberts concentrated upon mattresses, blue fibres for packing, blue yarns and cloth, and 'Limpet' flooring for railway carriages. Fireproofing and insulating materials for the railways became a major line. In 1931, a Roberts' engineer, Norman L. Dolbey, developed a major money-spinner for the group – sprayed Limpet asbestos. By this process, a mixture of asbestos, cement and atomised water was hosed onto ceilings and other surfaces, so providing a quick and economical method of fireproofing and sound-proofing railway carriages, buildings and other structures.

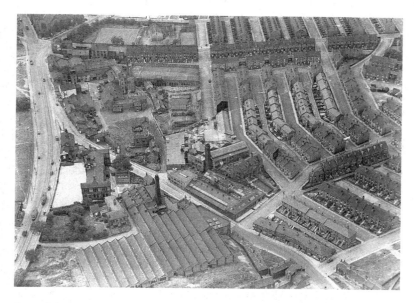

Figure 2.1 Aerial view of J.W. Roberts in 1949. The Armley factory is the small group of buildings in the centre of the photograph. Working conditions were so dusty that asbestosis and cancer were a fact of factory life. However, the proximity of houses and a school meant that residents and schoolchildren were also exposed to asbestos, thus sowing the seeds for one of Britain's worst industrial disasters. Asbestos dust can be seen lying on the factory roofs.

Source: (Courtesy of Woods Visual Communications, Bradford)

Roberts was wholly-owned by Turner & Newall, which after 1931 operated a multi-divisional structure. This type of organisation has been much admired by business historians and Turner & Newall were one of its first exponents. Major policy decisions were made at the centre in Rochdale (where TBA was the group headquarters), with the subsidiary, or unit company, acting as 'managers or agents'.[5] The daily running of the Leeds operations therefore remained in the hands of the Roberts' family. In the 1920s, these included the founder's sons, the most important of whom were Arthur C. Roberts and Wilfred N. Roberts. The latter stayed on the Roberts' board until his death in 1941, when the family connection ceased.[6] The commercial benefits of this structure were soon apparent. Blue asbestos was sold to other members of the group, such as Washington Chemical Co, with Roberts marketing the products of other unit companies. Although Roberts did not have the staff to exploit the spray process itself, it was able to licence it to other unit companies in the group – notably Newalls and Turners Asbestos Cement – and, of course, to other customers around the world.

Besides the multi-divisional structure, another feature of the Armley works should be emphasised. The factory was set in the heart of a working-class residential district, closely flanked by houses and a school, which greatly restricted expansion. The sloping site was never selected, nor laid out for asbestos manufacture; and the scale of its operations, despite various piecemeal additions, always remained relatively small. During and after the Second World War, for example, crude asbestos fibre was stored all over the West Riding, and at Armley one shift's output had to be despatched before the next shift could begin. The company occupied adjacent houses for office space, even though the total number of factory workers was small – 150 or less for much of the interwar period and only briefly surpassing 250 towards the end of the Second World War (see Table 2.1). This was only 2 per cent of the Turner & Newall workforce. In comparison, TBA's employees numbered over 3,000 by the 1950s in what was then the largest asbestos textile factory in the world. However, Roberts was a profitable company throughout most of its history, especially during the Second World War and early 1950s. By then the limitations of the site were becoming increasingly apparent. This fact, combined with the decline of the steam locomotive market, led in 1959 to the closure of the Armley factory. Roberts' activities (which now increasingly involved glass fibre and plastics) were transferred to a new Turner & Newall factory at Hindley Green, near Wigan, with new offices conveniently situated at Horwich, near Bolton. In 1970, Roberts was absorbed by another group company – Turners Asbestos Cement – to form what later became TAC Construction Materials Ltd. Thereafter Roberts existed in name only.

Occupational health background

Asbestos is an extremely tough material, with a tendency to split longitudinally into particles of invisible fineness. It has been long established that all types of asbestos can trigger pathological reactions if inhaled. In its *Annual Report* for 1898, the Factory Inspectorate highlighted the 'evil effects' of asbestos manufacture, because of its 'easily demonstrated danger to the health of the worker.'[7] By the 1920s, it was recognised that inhaling asbestos could cause asbestosis, a degenerative scarring of the

Table 2.1 Employees at J. W. Roberts, 1922–58

	Employees	Scheduled Employees	Spray/contract Employees
1922	37	32	
1923	43	37	
1924	48	42	
1925	79	72	
1926	93	86	
1927	120	110	
1928	146	136	
1929	150	140	
1930	152	140	
1931	106	94	2
1932	64	52	4
1933	92	76	6
1934	118	97	10
1935	129	102	15
1936	114	96	8
1937	128	107	11
1938	152	130	12
1939	140	118	10
1940	167	143	12
1941	181	151	18
1942	220		
1943	220		
1944	263		
1945			
1946			
1947			
1948	253		
1949	160		10
1950	130		10
1951	186		10
1952	214		
1953	183		
1954	180		
1955	193		
1956	183		
1957	162		
1958	171		

Source: 8/1855; 82/114–5. Memos on Employees at Roberts.

N.B. Data is missing for some years and there is some approximation, especially for contract workers, which after 1951 are probably included in the overall total. These figures also probably understate the total workforce, as other papers in the Turner & Newall archive suggest that directors and office staff were not included in this listing. The number of workers in 'scheduled' processes before 1931 is notional, as the scheduled areas were only officially created at that date.

lungs, which often led to death. In fact, the term 'asbestosis' had been coined by a pathologist involved in the first inquest on a British asbestos worker, who was employed by TBA and had died in 1924.[8]

When did this problem first appear at Armley? It is difficult to be precise, but certainly by the 1920s health had also become an issue at Roberts. In 1926, two Armley doctors, A. C. Haddow and Ian Grieve, noted asbestosis amongst Roberts' workers. In 1927, Grieve had produced a remarkable unpublished study of the disease, which identified more than a dozen workers with different stages of asbestosis, some of whom began dying soon after he had examined them.[9] For example, a 34-year-old Roberts' worker, William Leadbeater, died in March 1928 from pneumonia and asbestosis – an inquest verdict that Turner & Newall contested. By 1930, at least seven Roberts' workers had died of the disease (see Table 2.2); and the Roberts' directors told the Turner & Newall board that in the previous five years, ten workers had contracted asbestosis.[10]

In 1927 and 1929, the work of Haddow and Grieve had been discussed at British Medical Association meetings.[11] By then, Matthew Stewart, the Leeds University professor of pathology, had reported on the Roberts' cases in the medical press. He was also hired by the company as a pathologist in asbestosis cases. Stewart intended to research the problems at Roberts more fully, having been awarded a Medical Research Council grant for the purpose in 1929, but the company's opposition led to the scuppering of the scheme.[12] However, reports in the medical press about asbestosis had aroused official concern. In 1928, Dr Edward Merewether and Charles W. Price, Factory Inspectors at the Home Office, conducted a health and environmental study of the asbestos industry. Their sample survey, which was published in 1930, showed that the overall incidence of asbestosis in their cohort was about 35 percent; though after twenty years, four out of five workers still in the industry had the disease. The government quickly legislated for asbestosis with three measures. First, it introduced the Asbestos Industry Regulations (1931) to control dust in the industry. Second, a Medical Arrangements Scheme established a government Medical Board to examine workers annually, and suspend them from work if they developed asbestosis. Third, the asbestos industry was brought within the Workmen's Compensation Act by means of the Asbestos Industry (Asbestosis) Scheme, 1931. Workers disabled by asbestosis were to be offered compensation by the industry; and the dependants of those who died were to be offered a lump death benefit.

This was a pioneering piece of legislation in advance of other countries, and – whatever its failings – it was to remain in place until 1969. Thus, the 1931 Regulations, Medical and Asbestosis Schemes were to be

Table 2.2 Asbestosis Deaths at J.W. Roberts, 1927–30

Name	Years Employed	Job	Cause of Death	Post-mortem	Inquest
Harriet Slater (c. 1879–1927)	c. 24	Mattresses	Asbestosis	No	No
May Speke (c. 1893–1927)	c. 20	Mattresses	Asbestosis	Yes	No
Walter Leadbeater (c. 1894–1928)	14	Mattresses	Pneumonia/ asbestosis	Yes	Yes
Margaret Marsden (c. 1895–1928)	16	Mattresses	Asbestosis	Yes	Yes
Lily Hemsley (c. 1888–1929)	19	Mattresses	Asbestosis	Yes	Yes ('misadventure')
Abraham Jowett (c. 1891–1929)	6	Textiles	Heart failure/ pneumonia/ asbestosis	Yes	Yes ('natural causes')
Albert E.Witham (? – 1930)	c. 14	Mattresses	TB/asbestosis	Yes	Yes ('misadventure')

Sources: Turner & Newall compensation claims files; and I. M. D. Grieve, 'Asbestosis' (Edinburgh University MD thesis, 1927), which provides information on Hemsley, Leadbeater, Slater, and Speke. Some of these cases are also listed anonymously in E. R. A. Merewether, 'The Occurrence of Pulmonary Fibrosis and Other Pulmonary Affections in Asbestos Workers', Journal of Industrial Hygiene 12 (June 1930), pp. 239–57, 52. Merewether also lists another worker, 'JC', who died in 1928 and may have been employed at Roberts. Unfortunately, this individual died on a farm in the country and is therefore impossible to trace.

the basis for the protection and compensation offered to Roberts' workers at Armley. The 1931 statutes imposed a series of inter-related obligations upon the company, with which (at least ostensibly) it would have to comply. This article will now examine Roberts' and Turner & Newall's strategy to each of the three provisions in the government legislation.

Dust control at Roberts

The Asbestos Industry Regulations were framed in 1931 and came into effect in March 1933. They covered the main manufacturing processes – crushing, spinning and weaving, and the manufacture of leading asbestos products – and stipulated that local exhaust ventilation was to be utilised for them. Some processes, such as mattress-making (a Roberts' speciality) were singled out for special attention. Machinery was to be properly constructed so that dust could not escape and it was to be properly maintained. Workshops were to be kept clean and adequately lit, and impermeable sacks were to be introduced. Overalls and masks were to be used for the dustiest operations and some attempt was made to protect bystanders and young workers (the latter, for example, being banned from mattress-making and cleaning).

These dust Regulations, combined with the other measures, looked impressive. Yet they had some crucial limitations. After 1970, a quantitative safety threshold was set for asbestos dust by counting under an optical microscope the number of fibres per cubic centimetre of air.[13] However, in 1930 technology for measuring dust of any kind was limited and no quantitative limit was set. Merewether and Price had merely postulated that the dust level experienced by asbestos spinners should be the target for a dust threshold (which they labelled the 'dust datum'). This was despite the fact that, although spinners did appear to have a lower incidence of fibrosis, the disease still occurred amongst them. Another limitation reflected the circumstances in which the laws had been drafted. The statutes had been negotiated between the leading asbestos firms and the government. The industry had accepted the 'dust datum' (which at

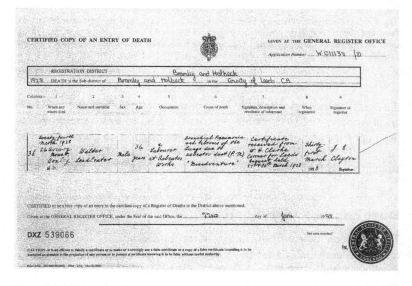

Figure 2.2 Walter Leadbeater was amongst the earliest documented cases of asbestosis at J. W. Roberts. Turner & Newall contested the medical diagnosis and declined to pay his widow, Doris, any compensation. She herself died from the same disease in 1931, leaving an orphaned son.

(continued)

CERTIFIED COPY OF AN ENTRY OF DEATH

GIVEN AT THE GENERAL REGISTER OFFICE

Application Number W011138/0

REGISTRATION DISTRICT Leeds South

1931 DEATH in the Sub-district of Bramley and Holbeck in the County of Leeds C.B.

Columns:–	1	2	3	4	5	6	7	8	9
No.	When and where died	Name and surname	Sex	Age	Occupation	Cause of death	Signature, description and residence of informant	When registered	Signature of registrar
4	Tenth March 1931 2 Aviary Grove Armley U.D.	Doris Leadbeater	Female	31 years	Mattress Hand at Asbestos works Widow of Walter Leadbeater a Labourer at Asbestos Works	Pulmonary asbestosis due to inhalation of asbestos dust during the course of her employment "Misadventure" P.M.	Certificate received from J. H. Milner Coroner for Leeds Inquest held 11th March 1931	Twelfth March 1931	J. E. Clayton Registrar

CERTIFIED to be a true copy of an entry in the certified copy of a Register of Deaths in the District above mentioned.

Given at the GENERAL REGISTER OFFICE, under the Seal of the said Office, the 23rd day of June 1998

DXZ 536961

See note overleaf

CAUTION:–It is an offence to falsify a certificate or to make or knowingly use a false certificate or a copy of a false certificate intending it to be accepted as genuine to the prejudice of any person or to possess a certificate knowing it to be false without lawful authority.

GENERAL REGISTER OFFICE ENGLAND

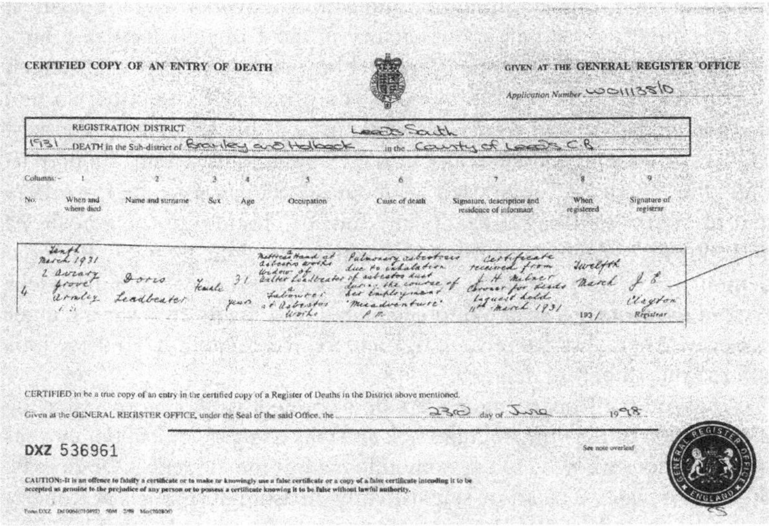

Figure 2.2 (continued)

the time was regarded as provisional), but only at a price. For its part, the government had agreed that the whole legislative framework only applied to asbestos jobs in the so-called 'scheduled areas' of the factories, where the main manufacturing processes were conducted. Workers outside the scheduled areas were excluded from dust protection, medical surveillance and often from compensation. One clause effectively excluded those laggers and factory workers (such as machinery cleaners) whose work in mixing asbestos materials was only 'occasional' – defined as no more than eight hours in any week. The Regulations also allowed the government to relax the rules at its discretion, which enabled the industry to lobby for exemptions in certain asbestos processes. Most crucially, the country's growing army of asbestos insulation workers (laggers) did not come within the 1931 legislation – an oversight which was to cost many workers their lives.

The effect of these measures can be seen at TBA in Rochdale, where the whole of the asbestos textiles division was scheduled – over 500 workers – but as many again were exempt. Roberts' workers were more fortunate: about eighty (most of the workforce) were initially within the Scheme and only a dozen or so office and ancillary staff, such as boilermen and cleaners, were not covered (see Table 2.1). On the other hand, this signified that the Midland Works was the dustiest and potentially most dangerous factory in the Turner & Newall group. Within its cramped confines, crude blue asbestos fibre was beaten ('opened') and then fluffed, blended and mixed with a cotton, so that it could be carded and spun – all recognised as highly dusty processes. Mattress-making generated dust well above the 'dust datum'. In preparing spray materials (composed of about 60 percent asbestos), workers had to shovel and bag a deadly mixture of crocidolite (or amosite)[14] and cement. Spraying this mixture – which was done by a few Roberts' demonstrators and contract workers, as well as many other licensees around the world – created unprecedented dust levels and was a danger not only to sprayers, but also to bystanders. Respirators in all these jobs offered only a partial defence.

What did the Roberts' managers do to protect its workforce after the introduction of the dust Regulations, and was its dust-control policy successful? First, we need to say something about the evidence. Obviously, there is no way we can now scientifically measure dust levels at Roberts in the 1920s and 1930s. The contemporary evidence is also scanty. Until the 1950s, no dust-counts were taken at Roberts, with the exception of a government-inspired attempt to discover dust levels for the spray process in 1938 (which showed that dust levels at both the 'dust datum' and during spraying were very high).[15] However, company reports, plans, drawings, photographs are available and these can be combined with other evidence, particularly from legal testimony, to give a picture of the dust situation at Armley. Finally, since all asbestos diseases have an extended latency – anything from five to over fifty years – then the situation at Armley in the 1930s and subsequent decades can be seen from later worker (and community) mortality.

During 1932, Turner & Newall began implementing these regulations through its newly-convened Asbestosis Committee at Rochdale. W. N. Roberts attended its first meeting in October 1931. Reflecting the decentralised structure of Turner & Newall, each unit company was asked to assess its problem areas and then report to the main board. Roberts' projected alterations were limited to installing ventilating plant for the looms, and the removal of four dust balloons (a job which was to be 'considered in due course').[16] Unfortunately, Roberts were one of the few companies that did not provide an estimate of costs. However, it was unlikely to have been very high. Turner & Newall spent about £10,000 on the initial dust suppression programme in 1932 – a year when group profits were over £360,000 after tax.

To be sure, some exhaust ventilation had already been installed at Armley in the late 1920s and this may have encouraged the company to believe that it was already doing enough. In 1929, Matthew Stewart had toured the factory and had praised the dust extraction system and the 'enormous pains' that the firm had taken.[17] In 1932, Turner & Newall's directors and medical advisers had described the Midland Works as 'fairly clean and . . . healthy'.[18] However, the company also admitted that discarded rubbish and fibre littered the workshops and clearly the Regulations were not always followed whole-heartedly. One idea of Wilfred N. Roberts was to turn dry mixing processes into wet ones, so that an exemption from the Regulations could be claimed. Another was to use casual labour to do the mixing and rotate the workforce, so that 'each new job gets fresh labourer.'[19] Thus the ruling over 'occasional' work could be confounded, even though rotation spread the risk among a greater number of men. W. N. Roberts seems to have preferred liberal quantities of water, rather than the expense of ventilation machinery. His ideas included keeping all the factory floors continually damp and soaking bags before they were moved.[20] The company meanwhile insisted that the spray process, invented in the very year of the government's legislation, was a 'wet' operation outside the Regulations – a point upon which the government agreed. The only protection workers had in this treacherous operation was the use of masks, which the company eventually made available after the 1930s – an admission that spraying was a very dusty job.

The scale and sophistication of Roberts' dust extraction plant was modest. In litigation in the 1990s, the dust-control system at Armley has been reconstructed in detail. Broadly, the major technique was forced-draft extraction to draw asbestos dust away at source to various collection plants. For example, in the early-stage processes (such as milling or fiberising), suction pipes were used to extract dust; the same method that was used in the spinning and mattress rooms. Not all dust was sucked into collecting points (which had to be cleaned out regularly); some fans simply exhausted the dust into the streets. There was also some reliance on natural or 'static' dust extraction, through vents on the roof (such as those in the card room) or through open doors and windows.

Thus, dust extraction 'served to make no more than a contribution to countering the internal dust problem.'[21] Workers testified that in the early 1950s, the factory was still very dusty. In one of the sheds, suction pipes removed the bulk of the dust from the disintegrator, but one worker has stated that there was still 'dust in the air like fog all day and every day.'[22] In the carding shop, dust extraction was deficient and some machines had no exhaust hoods. One worker there, who developed asbestosis after only about five years, found it difficult to see from one end of the room to the other.[23] Until the Midland Works closed, mattresses were still made in the traditional manner by manually stuffing waste asbestos into woven asbestos bags and then bashing them into shape on a long table. Although damping was encouraged and the first-floor mattress room had exhaust ventilation, the work generated clouds of dust. Unfilled mattresses had to be collected from a dusty store and when finished had to be manhandled along a corridor: there was no exhaust ventilation for these jobs and the 'whole corridor was dusty. It was swept with a brush, but . . . it was never cleaned properly.'[24] All manual workers were covered in dust by the end of their shifts: hence nicknames, such as 'abominable snowman' or 'featherlegs'.

Dust was not only a problem inside the factory. So heavy were emissions from the Roberts' extractor fans, that the dust can clearly be seen on the factory roof from an aerial photograph taken in 1949. Roberts' workers brought dust home on their clothes. In the local streets, the pavements and even the inside of some of the houses (including the lofts) were contaminated with asbestos, while children played amongst sacks of blue asbestos that Roberts had stacked in a loading bay accessible from the street. In the words of one resident, it was 'as though we were practically eating dust . . . I have seen it blow around like a snowstorm.'[25]

One director admitted that after the Second World War: 'There were undoubtedly areas where the dust count exceeded our "norm" . . . by a wide margin.'[26] Yet the Roberts' management made little attempt to improve conditions. In fact, they regarded dust as an inevitable feature of factory life and doggedly resisted any attempts to extend the 1931 Regulations. These statutory orders were regarded as 'impracticable'. When, in the early 1950s, the company began to realise it would have little defence against common law actions, the company tried to persuade the Home Office to alter the Regulations. Turner & Newall did not want to tighten the safety measures! Instead, they demanded a qualifying clause, so that exhaust equipment was to prevent the escape of dust only '*so far as reasonably practicable.*'[27] Fortunately for the workforce, no such amendment was ever passed. Meanwhile, in the 1940s both Turner & Newall and the Roberts' management fought a long and successful rearguard action against the government to prevent spraying becoming a scheduled operation.[28]

Medical surveillance

With inadequate dust control, workers would obviously need to rely on the medical and compensation scheme. The Medical Arrangements

Scheme was one of the non-negotiable elements in the government's asbestosis package. The Medical Board, which examined and suspended workers, was an independent government body, whose medical reports were confidential (unless the worker deemed otherwise), and whose decisions were final. Turner & Newall and its unit companies were relegated to the role of making workers available for examination, providing suitable facilities at the works for the examinations, and funding the Scheme (which it did under protest). At TBA, a part-time medical adviser was employed by the company in the 1930s, and in 1949 Dr John Knox was appointed as a full-time medical officer. However, none of the other unit companies provided a doctor. Roberts made occasional use of a local doctor for any company examinations; and the only other medical facility at the works was an ambulance room. Knox, however, did sometimes visit Armley.

The relationship between the Medical Board and Turner & Newall has been examined in detail elsewhere.[29] The Board did not prove entirely effective: asbestosis was not always easy to diagnose and the government medical officers were often reluctant to suspend workers, both because it took away their livelihood and because it upset the company. The Board operated a very conservative policy, which resulted in a relatively low number of suspensions and 'official' asbestosis deaths.

What was the situation at Roberts? The Turner & Newall archive shows that after 1931 at least 98 Roberts' workers were suspended with asbestos disease, almost all with exposure at Armley. Most of these individuals (and others who were not suspended) died from their occupational disease, because 127 asbestos-related deaths were recorded in the files. These figures are certainly underestimates. The records of Roberts' are not always complete and the company had a reputation for bad medical record-keeping.[30] It has anyway long been recognised that all asbestos-disease statistics are underestimates, even after the 1960s.[31] The conservative policy of the Medical Board must also be borne in mind. A worker did not have to be suspended by the Board to suffer and die from asbestos disease – a fact which accounts for some of the discrepancy between suspensions and deaths. With this in mind, it is likely that the number of suspensions at Armley was well over a hundred and the death toll certainly in excess of 127 between 1931 and the 1970s.

It is beyond the scope of this article to examine the full medical picture at Armley. However, a number of brief observations can be made, using the J. W. Roberts' compensation files (about 155 of which have survived). First, Roberts was easily the most hazardous unit company in the group. Between 1931 and 1958, about 270 Turner & Newall workers were suspended with asbestosis; the figure for Roberts was about 71. In other words, the Armley factory was responsible for well over a third (about 38 per cent) of Turner & Newall's asbestosis cases; yet Roberts only accounted for 1–2 per cent of the group's employees. Second, over 80 workers from about 155 cases developed asbestosis (and/or asbestos cancers) even though they had started work *after* 1932 – thus demonstrating the ineffectiveness of the dust Regulations. Third, many workers developed fatal diseases after only a very brief period of asbestos exposure. In the 155 Roberts' case files are the records of some 59 individuals who developed asbestos disease in ten or less years' exposure. In some workers, exposure was less than five years. To give only one example, William H. Evans, a fiberiser who had started at Roberts in 1947, died in 1982 from heart failure and asbestosis (and cancer of the prostate) after only 20 months' work in the factory. A review of cases from the other Turner & Newall factories shows that not only were individuals more likely to develop asbestos disease at Roberts, they were also likely to develop it more rapidly.

Roberts' history also provides important evidence of the occupational cancer risk caused by asbestos. The mineral not only increases the risk of lung cancer (especially in smokers), it can also trigger mesothelioma, a virulent cancer of the lining of the chest (pleurae) or abdomen (peritoneum).[32] The medical community increasingly regarded lung cancer as an occupational hazard of asbestos workers from the early 1940s, with TBA first being alerted to the trend through inquests on its Rochdale workers and through private medical research in America (where T&N had a subsidiary). In 1955, (Sir) Richard Doll, a leading cancer epidemiologist, confirmed the link in a landmark study on TBA workers. Roberts' workers also showed a relatively high incidence of lung cancer; there are at least 28 documented cases of carcinoma of the lung (usually in association with asbestosis) amongst its workers between the 1940s and 1970s. The first Roberts' lung cancer/asbestosis case under the Asbestosis Scheme died in 1944. By the following year, when another Roberts' worker died from the same diseases, pathologists in Leeds agreed that the asbestos had led to the development of the cancer.[33]

The scientific proof that asbestos could cause mesothelioma was not published until 1960s. However, it is interesting to note that postmortem reports in the Roberts' files allow us to identify retrospectively a few probable mesotheliomas from the 1940s and 1950s. For example, between 1945 and 1946 there were three cases of carcinomatosis of the peritoneum. To what extent pathologists linked this with asbestos is debatable. But when Leeds pathologist M. J. Stewart found a cancer of the lining of the chest in the body of a suspended Roberts' worker in 1949, he wrote in his diary – 'tumour a pleural mesothelioma?'.[34]

Compensation

The limited success of dust control and medical surveillance meant that many sick workers and their families depended heavily on the final component of government support – financial compensation. Two schemes operated while the Midland Works was active. Between 1931 and 1948, workmen's compensation was paid out under the Asbestosis Scheme and benefits were calculated according to the worker's pre-sickness earnings and the costs were met by the employer (or their insurers). After 1948, under the National Insurance (Industrial Injuries) Act, this method was replaced by one in which benefits were solely related to the level of disability – in other words, the benefits for a manager were the same as for a labourer – and the costs were met by the state.

Whichever method operated, there was little difference in levels of payment, which invariably failed to compensate the worker fully. Under the Asbestosis Scheme, partial incapacity brought a payment of half the difference between a worker's present wage (or assessed earning capacity) and his pre-suspension earnings; compensation for complete incapacity could not exceed fifty per cent of the worker's average weekly earnings. No compensation payment could exceed 30s [£1.50] a week. Compensation remained low after 1948, when total disability brought a state compensation payment of £2 15s 0d [£2.75].

Even the maximum payment under the Asbestosis Scheme of 30s a week was well below most workers' wages and penalised the better paid (as all workers were treated by the Asbestosis Scheme as alike, whether skilled/unskilled or married/single). There was no extra allowance for dependants or for medical costs. Roberts' compensation files in the 1930s show this reduction in wages quite clearly. George T. Wilson, a mattress beater, earned about £152 in the year before he was totally disabled by asbestosis, but his compensation payment between 1932 and 1940 was only about £76 a year. William Birch (1892–1955), a disintegrator, was suspended as partially disabled in 1951: his £5 12s. 3d [£5.61] sickness benefit and disability pension was well below his former average weekly wage of £7 9s. 11d [£7.50]. Generally, the Roberts' experience confirms what other studies on worker's compensation have revealed: the cost of industrial compensation did not fall entirely on the employer. The worker, too, paid part of the cost, even though he was usually blameless.[35]

TBA found ways of softening the economic blow of suspension, especially if the worker was classed as only partially disabled. The factory was large enough to permit sick workers to be transferred to less strenuous jobs outside the scheduled areas, such as in the warehouse. At Roberts, however, the size of the factory made such transfers more problematical: William Birch, mentioned above, was allowed the dubious privilege by the Medical Board of continuing working at the less strenuous (but scarcely less dusty) job of fibre-opening.[36] More often sick workers left the company. Their prospects were grim, especially for those who left the industry in the 1930s and 1940s. Most asbestotics were dead by their mid-fifties and their 'asbestos widows' and dependants could then expect at most a lump sum death payment.

This sum was set by the Workman's Compensation Act (1925) at a maximum of £300,[37] though extra amounts for dependant children could raise this to £600. These sums did not represent punitive damages, which even in the 1990s cannot be claimed through industrial compensation. Nor were these sums very generous for families that had often lost their main breadwinner. By the late 1930s and early 1940s, some of the better-paid Roberts' workers could earn £200 to £300 a year; by the 1950s, £400 or more. For most, the maximum lump sum was only two years' wages. By the 1960s (when the lump sum limit was still only £400) death benefit for the dependants of workers who had been suspended with asbestosis was derisory. Even worse, as Table 2.3 reveals, only ten cases from Roberts' total of 36 suspensions/deaths under the Asbestosis Fund merited an award of £300 or more. The claims files show that at least a dozen received nothing, or merely funeral costs.

Numerous factors hindered dependants claiming the full sum, or indeed any sum. Payment was calculated by the government's statutory formula. From this amount, the firm could legitimately deduct the compensation already paid to any suspended worker up to a maximum of £100. Thus, in the case of suspended and compensated workers, Turner & Newall was partially reimbursed for its costs and the maximum that dependants could claim was often £200.

Workers who had left the industry before the introduction of the Asbestosis Scheme in May 1931 were not eligible for compensation. Mrs M. A. Ashton, a 36-year-old Roberts' worker who had left shortly before the implementation of the legislation, died with asbestosis in 1934 after childbirth. Although her case was put before the Turner & Newall board, there is no record of any compensation paid on her behalf. Workers employed outside the scheduled areas could not claim compensation either. Roberts' cashier, Arthur Dobson, died in 1934 from asbestosis and

Name	Service	Job	Suspended	Cause of Death	Death Payment
Edith Dobson (c. 1888–1937)	1905–17; 1923–32	Textiles/mattresses	1932	Asbestosis	£55
Mary J. Hagerty (c. 1888–1943)	1912–32	Mattresses	1932	Bright's disease/asbestosis	£15 (funeral costs)
Eva A. Harrison (1900–51)	1917–32	Mattresses/samples	1932	Lung cancer/asbestosis	£55 (funeral costs/ex – gratia)
George T. Wilson (1886–1942)	1913–32	Mattresses	1932	Asbestosis	£200
Akrill Dobson (c. 1904–34)	1924–33	Textiles	1933	Asbestosis/TB	£100
Martha Jackson (c. 1902–1953)	1920–46	Textiles	1934	Asbestosis	£1 per week ex – gratia
Hilda McLean (c. 1902–1949)	1917–33	Mattresses	1934	Asbestosis	£15 (funeral costs)
Emmeline O'Connor (c. 1888–1937)	c. 1910–32	Textiles	1934	Heart failure/asbestosis	None
Amy Osborne (c. 1886–1940)	1903–21; 1923–32	Textiles	1934	Valvular heart disease	None
William Atha (c. 1897 – ?)	c. 1929–35	Mattresses	1935	Asbestosis	£125 (paid while alive)
Dorothy Bell (1906–75)	1919–48	Textiles	1935	Asbestosis/coronary heart disease	None
Frederick H. Fallowes (1902–49)	1925–35	Fibre plant	1935	Asbestosis/pleural sarcoma (?mesothelioma)	£200
Rowland Nicholls (c. 1908–1946)	1926–35	Labouring/mattresses	1935	Insanity/asbestosis	None
Doris Sanderson (1906–36)	1924–34	Textiles	1935	TB/Asbestosis	£250
Arthur W. Slater (1877–1941)	1927–39	Mattresses	1935	Asbestosis	£166
Frederick Tring (1891–1954)	1911–35	Labouring/mattresses	1935	Asbestosis	£300
Lawrence W. Wallis (1873–1955)	1926–31, 1933–5	Mattresses/fibre plant	1935	Asbestosis	£300
William Wood (1890–1944)	1927–35	Mattresses	1935	Lung cancer/asbestosis	None

(Continued)

Table 2.3 (Continued)

Name	Service	Job	Suspended	Cause of Death	Death Payment
Annie Asquith (1896–1978)	1929?–1939	Textiles/ cleaning	1936	Cor pulmonale/ bronchitis/ asbestosis	None
Joseph Macbeth (1891–1949)	1927–36	Textiles	1936	Flu/pneumonia/ myocarditis. No inquest.	None
Lily Fowler (1904–43)	1930–2; 1937–8	Mattresses	1938(TB)	TB/asbestosis	None
Arthur Greensmith (1897–1943)	1919–21; 1924–43	Mattresses/ textiles	1939	Asbestosis	£363
Eliza A. Collison (1891–1964)	1927–42	Textiles	1942	Asbestosis	£30 (funeral costs)
John H. Young (1902–43)	1927–42	Fibre plant	1942	Asbestosis	£337
Harold S. Kaye (1903–52)	1927–43	Textiles	1943	Asbestosis/cancer peritoneum (?mesothelioma)	£300
Ellis Taylor (c. 1902–1963)	c. 1928–43	Textiles	1943	Lung cancer/asbestosis	£300
Joseph S. Cowlam (1887–1949)	1934–44	Textiles/ mattresses	1944	Lung cancer No inquest	£15 (funeral costs)
Joseph Greensmith (c. 1885–1946)	1919–44	Textiles	1944	Carcinomatosis peritoneum (?mesothelioma)/ asbestosis	None
Thomas Kendrew (1906–55)	1921–45	Mattresses	1945	Lung cancer/asbestosis	£50 ex-gratia + funeral costs
Alice Kitchen (c. 1903–68)	c. 1930–45	Mattresses	1945	Carcinomatosis/ovarian cancer	None
John S. Lister (1907–49)	1924–45	Maintenance	1945	Asbestosis	£403
William H. Jagger (1905–53)	1919–46	Mattresses	1946	Lung cancer/asbestosis	£300
Fred Lister (1910–66)	1927–46+(intermittent)	Textiles	1946	Asbestosis	£15 (funeral costs)
Mary J. Ritchie (c. 1896–1955)	1927–39; 1944–6	Textiles	1946	Suicide (drowning)	None
Joseph Thompson (1901–52)	1932–40	Textiles	1947	Asbestosis	£500 ex-gratia (+£30 funeral costs)
William Davies (c. 1901–66)	1924–48	Textiles	1948	Asbestosis	£300

tuberculosis after thirty years' service. His widow received no compensation; though she did when their son, Akrill, died. The latter, a carder, died from asbestosis and tuberculosis in the same year, eliciting a payment from Roberts of £100. Workers who had left the scheduled areas for more than three years before developing asbestosis (or after 1939, more than five years) were also not eligible.

Even for workers within the Scheme, compensation was not a foregone conclusion. The death payment came only at the end of various complex legal and medical processes. These usually began with a post-mortem and inquest, at which the dead worker's dependants would be confronted by Roberts' managers, legal counsel and medical expert. After 1943, Turner & Newall hired Professor M. J. Stewart (now one of the leading pathologists in the country) as their consultant in asbestosis cases. Usually, the company's main concern was to avoid liability and minimise the role of asbestos as the main cause of death. Asbestosis was sometimes accompanied by broncho-pneumonia and heart failure; or death could be caused by tuberculosis or asbestos-related lung cancer and mesothelioma (which were not yet official industrial diseases).[38] The lack of a clear-cut diagnosis sometimes allowed the company (and the coroner) to shift the blame away from asbestos. When Mary Hagerty died from Bright's disease accelerated by asbestosis, the company argued that the former disease was primarily to blame. When William Wood died of asbestosis and lung cancer in 1944, Turner & Newall argued that 'asbestosis . . . [was] . . . not the cause of death'.[39]

Even if the coroner reached a 'death by industrial disease' verdict, compensation could still be blocked. Inquests were not legally binding and Turner & Newall still required – as they were entitled to do – a Medical Board certificate officially confirming an asbestosis death. Obtaining such a certificate was the job of the relatives and they then had to make a claim to the company by the formal channels. This was another expense for claimants, who had to pay £2 2s 0d [£2.10] of which £1 10s 0d [£1.50] was refunded if the certificate was issued. Even if they jumped through that hoop, they could still be felled by the issue of dependency. As we have stated, the lump sum death payment was not a punitive award against the company; it was intended to compensate a family for the income forfeited by the death of its main breadwinner. Again, it was not an automatic payment, as a lump sum was only payable to those who could *prove* dependency. Even if they had secured a Medical Board certificate, dependants could find themselves in another round of correspondence, negotiations and costs (this time for birth and marriage certificates) over their claim for dependency. Generally, only unemployed widows and children under 16 were recognised as truly dependent and eligible for compensation.

Turner & Newall and its subsidiaries often preferred to settle matters with an *ex-gratia* payment. Sometimes the *ex-gratia* was paid as a small weekly pension each week; or as a sum to cover legal costs or funeral expenses; or occasionally the *ex-gratia* would be paid as a lump sum at death. Lump sum *ex-gratias* were relatively rare and were usually only made on sympathetic grounds if it was decided that 'officially' there was no claim or liability, but that there were mitigating circumstances. This was not a statutory obligation and was paid at the company's discretion. The *ex-gratia* payment was a paternalistic device, which satisfied the company's charitable instincts and often aroused gratitude in the recipient. It was 'without prejudice', subject to annual review, and it was made clear that legal action by relatives could result in its complete withdrawal. When a suspended Roberts' worker, Walter Talbot, died from a clear case of asbestosis in 1972, the company ignored the solicitor's claim for a lump sum and paid the widow £2 per week *ex-gratia*. The solicitor was asked to bear in mind that this was subject to annual review.[40]

How much compensation did Roberts pay? Table 2.4 shows the status of the Asbestosis Fund in 1957, shortly before the Armley factory closed. Turner & Newalls' total compensation payment from the Fund was £97,279, a relatively small sum considering that in the period between 1931 and 1957 the company had made profits after tax of about £55 million. The comparison between Roberts' compensation payments and those of other Turner & Newall factories is also instructive: its tiny workforce was responsible for a quarter of the compensation costs.

Table 2.4 Asbestosis Fund Statistics, 1957

Company	Contributions £	Compensation £	Balance £	Current Claims
Turner Bros Asbestos	88,284	59,825	28,459	16
J.W. Roberts	38,259	25,880	12,379	7
Washington Chemical Co	8,367	6,272	2,095	3
Turners Asbestos Cement	11,846	5,302	6,544	3
	146,756	97,279	49,477	29

Source: T&N Board Papers, Asbestosis Fund Report for Year to 30 Sept. 1957.

Aftermath

In the early 1970s, as asbestos diseases began attracting national attention, a Turner & Newall public relations officer wrote: 'I hope very much
indeed that we are never called upon to discuss Armley in the public
arena.'[41] At that time, it must have seemed likely that the factory's past
would be forgotten. The old Midland Works was soon occupied by other
tenants and the only other reminder of the past in Armley was a few
remaining asbestosis cases. But Roberts would return to haunt Turner &
Newall.

In 1978, Leeds City Council alerted Turner & Newall to the fact
that the old factory was contaminated to 'a considerable extent' with
blue asbestos.[42] The company began a £13,000 clean-up, accepting a
moral though not a legal responsibility. Worse was to follow. Asbestos
exposure – even in small doses for a few months – also causes mesothelioma, a cancer that can have a latency up to fifty years or more. In
1988, the Leeds coroner Philip Gill expressed concern at the number of
mesothelioma deaths – 22 between 1977 and 1988 – referred for inquest.
Richard Taylor, a reporter for the *Yorkshire Evening Post*, traced the
deaths to Roberts' factory. The newspaper then began a series of reports
under the headline, 'The Armley Asbestos Tragedy'. In November 1988,
John Battle, the MP for Leeds West, demanded a government inquiry
into the deaths – a call supported by Leeds City Council. This was
rejected by the Under-Secretary of State, Patrick Nicholls, who argued
that an enquiry would cause needless concern, that it was impossible to
discover what had been done at Roberts, and that no one could then have
imagined that asbestos would have harmed residents.[43] Others took a less
resigned view. In the following month, Yorkshire Television transmitted
a documentary on Roberts, entitled 'Too Close to Home'.[44] It emphasised the environmental dangers and provided details of 'bystander'
mesothelioma deaths. Dust from the factory, especially from workers'
clothing, had been heavy enough to cause asbestosis and cancer amongst
residents and workers' relatives. For example, the family of John Young
was hit particularly hard. A Roberts' disintegrator, Young died in 1943
from asbestosis. His wife, Doris, died from mesothelioma in 1969; and
both his twin sons, David and Hubert, had also developed asbestosis by
the 1980s. One of the twins died of asbestosis in 1993. Apart from John
Young himself, none of the family had worked with asbestos. Ominously,
mesothelioma was also occurring amongst individuals who merely lived
near the factory, yet had never worked there themselves nor had relatives

working there. Mesothelioma appeared, for example, amongst individuals whose main exposure had occurred as children whilst playing in the streets near the factory.

In 1992, Leeds Council launched an Asbestos Survey of 290 properties in Armley, which reported that 90 per cent of them were contaminated to some extent with asbestos dust. This report had a predictable impact on property prices. By this time, the Turner & Newall archive had been made available by Chase Manhattan Bank during its legal action against the company. This provided further publicity about Armley;[45] and enabled victims to mount successful challenges against Turner & Newall. In 1996, an 'asbestos widow', Evelyn Margereson, and June Hancock, a mesothelioma victim whose mother had also died from this disease, were awarded £115,000 damages against T&N. This was a test case for others claiming environmental injuries from asbestos, as Margereson's husband, Arthur, and June Hancock had been exposed to the dust as children and had never worked at Roberts.[46] June Hancock died in the following year.

What is the final death toll at Armley? It is impossible to give a precise answer, not least because victims are still dying. Attempts have been made to provide a rough count in recent litigation and a figure of 93 asbestosis cases has been mentioned.[47] However, this is an underestimate. The company files note 127 deaths, mostly before the 1970s. But there are about two dozen further compensation cases, where death from an asbestos-related disease was the probable outcome, though it has not actually been recorded in the files. A total of about 150 deaths may be more realistic. But we need to add to this total the mesothelioma deaths (both Roberts' workers and bystanders) between 1971 and 1987, which were identified by Dr Lorna Arblaster and her colleagues.[48] That study found 64 deaths from mesothelioma relating to J. W. Roberts at Armley. When these are added to our previous total (discounting about ten overlapping cases), the number of Roberts' workers, their relatives or Armley residents, who have died from asbestos-related disease is 200 people or more.

Retrospect

The mortality resulting from Roberts' factory vies with that of some of Britain's worst industrial disasters. What were the most important factors at the root of the tragedy?

Historical circumstance played a part. Roberts' legacy included a site that was too small and cramped; a factory close to houses, busy streets

Figure 2.4 June Hancock (1936–97). As a child, Mrs Hancock played in the asbestos-contaminated streets round the Roberts' Factory. In the early 1990s, she was stricken with the asbestos cancer, mesothelioma (the same disease that had already killed her mother). She fought to win compensation from T&N, travelling to the High Court and later the Court of Appeal while in constant pain from an illness she knew to be terminal. T&N tried to evade liability but were eventually ordered by the courts to pay her £65,000 in damages. However, the knowledge that the landmark legal case (the first for environmental asbestos exposure) could lead to claims from other sufferers, gave June Hancock much greater satisfaction.

Source: Courtesy of *Yorkshire Post Newspapers Ltd*

and a school; and a raw material that was to prove far more dangerous than anyone could have imagined. Even worse, Roberts specialised in crocidolite, which after the 1960s was believed to be the most lethal of the commercial asbestos types. All these determinants were in place by the 1920s, sowing the seeds for a future health problem even before the government had legislated for asbestosis. Nevertheless, the scale of the Armley problem owed much to management and regulatory failings.

The sheer lack of constraint on the management in matters of health and safety is striking. The 1931 Regulations were intended to be 'provisional', and yet it is clear that between the 1930s and 1950s there was little chance that the asbestos legislation would be tightened. The Factory Inspectors visited the Midland Works, as they toured other Turner & Newall factories, yet the company were never censured or prosecuted for their lack of compliance with the Regulations. An older director recalled that: 'in my years at Armley we did not once receive any official adverse criticism from the Factory Inspectors who made regular visits sometimes five or six a year.'[49] It was almost as though the Regulations did not exist. Ironically, one Roberts' director, John Waddell, who later became chairman of TBA, had been a Factory Inspector for thirteen years before he joined the company. The Inspectorate itself admitted in 1956 that national compliance with the asbestos Regulations was sometimes 'extremely variable' and enforcement by the Inspectors 'difficult' and at times 'impossible'.[50] Yet transgressions were clearly not punished, as there were only two prosecutions under the 1931 Regulations: that was in 1935 and 1936, when two separate convictions (neither of which involved Turner & Newall) brought total fines of £23 plus costs. Hardly surprisingly, Armley was not unique. Another asbestos health blackspot was at Cape Asbestos's Acre Mill factory at Hebden Bridge, another Yorkshire town to the west of Leeds. This factory operated over a similar time-period as Roberts, until its closure in 1970. An Ombudsman's report on Acre Mill, published in 1976, highlighted an appalling record of bureaucratic muddle and ineptitude by the Factory Inspectorate extending over decades.[51] Not only were the asbestos regulations constantly breached, but the Inspectors failed to prosecute the firm. Here the death toll has so far surpassed 400.

Doubtless, many reasons can be advanced for this weak regulatory hand: in the Depression of the 1930s, workers needed jobs; during the Second World War, strategic concerns pushed health issues into the background; and during the 1950s, expanding markets likewise placed the emphasis on production. The Factory Inspectorate was often chronically understaffed and the volume of work was sometimes overwhelming, especially in dusty trades such as coal, where the death toll in accidents and lung fibrosis was numerically far higher than asbestos-related deaths.

Meanwhile, trade unions played only a limited role in negotiating better working conditions. The T&N compensation files for Roberts' workers are devoid of any signs of union activity (though those for TBA show that the unions may have played a limited role behind the scenes in providing and funding legal advice). To be sure, legal action was not usually a serious option, as it was constrained by cost and by the limitation period for tort claims – which meant that common law injury actions had to commence within six years from the last relevant exposure.[52] Because of the long latency of asbestos disease, most legal actions before the 1960s were 'statute-barred.' This was aside from the heavy costs of such actions. Not surprisingly, common law claims against Turner & Newall were rare. Before the 1970s, there was only one Roberts' common law claim: that was by the relatives of Thomas G. McDonald, who died in 1951 from tuberculosis and asbestosis after only eight years as a fibre mixer. An out-of-court settlement was reached for £1,000 plus costs.

Yet, it is also clear that many workers did not feel inclined to pursue Turner & Newall in the courts. There was some element of 'bargaining' at Armley. On the one hand, the company did what they felt they should as regards dust control given the nature of the product and the site; on the other, they reserved any extra expenditure for the higher than average wages needed to attract workers given the dusty conditions, and for the payment of compensation. Some workers seem to have accepted an element of risk for extra money, though this was not based on complete information about the hazards. An old Roberts' mattress-maker recalled: 'The pay we received at the factory was more than that I would have received had I had a sewing job. The reason I went to Roberts was because I wanted to earn more money to get married. It was generally thought that working there was a little bit dangerous, but no one had any idea it was as dangerous as it is now known.'[53]

Another strategy that allowed the company to manufacture a health hazard was paternalism. It was this that Roberts' own directors identified as the main reason for the firm's commercial success, despite the 'absence of any of those features which today are considered essential to a well-planned and efficient production unit.' They argued that 'it was not the patchwork of buildings, ancient and modern, which achieved this [success], but the generations of men and women who worked in them and responded to the imaginative leadership of Arthur Clifford Roberts and Wilfred Norman Roberts. Out of this interaction, came a sense of community or family feeling which, surviving the difficult years' of the depression could still be felt at Midland Works after the brothers had passed on, even in fact, to the very end.'[54]

This 'spirit' of Armley was not all management hyperbole. Local doctor Ian Grieve noted in 1927 that staff welfare at Roberts was more generous than elsewhere: a heavy three-course meal was supplied daily for a few pence and when an employee was ill, money, food, and wine might be given, and even, occasionally, doctor's fees.[55] Many Roberts' workers and dependants (though certainly not all) accepted their *ex-gratias* and reduced lump sums without protest: indeed in some cases, they accepted the company's hand-outs with profuse thanks. Not until the 1970s – well after Roberts had closed – did the organisation of asbestos victims' action-groups and media pressure signify a change of attitude in society, when sick workers began fighting for their rights. But even then, there was no workers' 'revolt' in Armley. A Turner & Newall manager visited several disabled Roberts' workers in 1977, partly with the ulterior motive of 'uncovering any plots' against the company for better compensation payments. He told his bosses: 'Everyone was pleased to see me and we "raked over" the past and enjoyed our conversations. Mostly the talk was of anything but asbestosis and illness.'[56] He concluded that the 'possibility of organised action from Armley employees seems improbable.' When that action did come in the 1990s, it was organised more by external parties – by the media, bankers and lawyers – than by those directly involved.

For business historians, this study offers some intriguing findings for those who regard decentralisation as a model. The multi-divisional structure at Turner & Newall was certainly highly effective at generating profits,[57] but it also allowed poor working conditions to flourish unchecked. Situated some fifty miles from Rochdale, where TBA's working conditions were much better, J. W. Roberts survived as a Victorian relic. Newcomers noted the old-fashioned working conditions and the dirt and disorder. In 1956, a sales trainee remarked on the lack of urgency in devising new ideas: 'If ideas come along, all well and good, but nobody seemed to take it upon themselves to do any active thinking on the subject.'[58] This mentality was made worse by the impending closure of the factory.

These problems certainly did not develop through ignorance. In 1949, the Turner & Newall directors admitted that working conditions at Armley were 'well below current standards'.[59] Workers' mortality and compensation payments at Roberts were reported annually to the main Rochdale board through the Asbestosis Fund. Roberts' directors also sat on the Turner & Newall board; and likewise the Rochdale directors attended the local board meetings at Leeds. But the excessive asbestosis suspension and death rate at Roberts aroused little comment or action: in fact, the only action that the main board took was to adjust slightly Roberts' subscriptions to the Asbestosis Fund, so that it could pay relatively more than the other unit companies to cover Armley's higher incidence of disease.

Ironically, the multi-divisional structure also hindered Armley workers and residents in their quest for compensation. The latency of asbestos disease meant that by the time many individuals became ill, Turner & Newall's precise relationship with Roberts had become hazy. Turner & Newall directors gave the impression that Roberts had ceased to exist and that the company's records were 'extremely scanty – and . . . largely confined to basic employee record cards.[60] In fact, the company was assembling and indexing, on instruction by the American courts, a vast historical archive in Manchester. When the Margereson/Hancock case came to trial in 1995, the company still denied having any documents on the grounds that what belonged to Roberts had nothing to do with them.[61] Turner & Newall initially declined to admit that its activities and liabilities were coterminous with those of its old unit company. In fact, Roberts existed as a shell: it had no assets, but Turner & Newall retained 'power' over its records, which, as Chase Manhattan Bank so gleefully demonstrated, were hardly 'scanty'. Some 27,000 Roberts' documents were eventually released a few weeks before the Leeds trial, hardly allowing the plaintiffs' solicitors time to read them. T&N were severely criticised by the trial judge for these tactics, which he thought 'reflected a wish to contest these claims by any means possible, legitimate or otherwise, so as to wear [the plaintiffs] down by attrition.'[62]

T&N lost that case, opening the way for similar claims. By 1997, crippled by its asbestos-disease liabilities, T&N was taken over by an American engineering company. It was a striking reminder that companies, especially those involved in the manufacture of hazardous materials, neglect occupational health and safety at their peril. For business historians, the Armley asbestos episode also has important lessons: it demonstrates that the study of business ethics, corporate behaviour, and the impact of industry on the environment can be as revealing as more traditional approaches which are only concerned with dynamic entrepreneurs, business structures, competitive advantage and technological innovation. Roberts' strategies show that corporations are also about short-term expediency, the manipulation of information, and the pursuit of profits at the expense of occupational and environmental health.[63]

Acknowledgements

This article draws on a project initiated by Professor David Jeremy and continued by the author, with funding from the Wellcome Trust. Dr Philip Hansen contributed to the analysis of the compensation files. I am particularly grateful to Michael O'Connor, vice-president and senior associate counsel of Chase Manhattan Bank, and his assistant Eric Rytter, for access to the Bank's microfilm of T&N documents. John Pickering and Adrian Budgen kindly provided relevant transcripts from the Margereson/Hancock trial. Professor Nick Wikeley has provided help and offprints at various times. Dr Lorna Arblaster and Dr Morris Greenberg not only provided advice in the preparation of this article, but also supplied material from their own extensive researches into Roberts' medical history.

Afterword

Geoffrey Tweedale

The events at the J. W. Roberts' factory at Armley form one of the bleakest episodes in British industrial history. However, in the late 1990s – when I completed my article – the story seemed to be ending in a victory of sorts for surviving victims and campaigners.[64] June Hancock had won her landmark legal decision against asbestos manufacturer T&N for environmental asbestos exposure. In 1997, The June Hancock Mesothelioma Fund had been established as the UK's first and largest mesothelioma charity. By 2000, the importation and production of asbestos products were banned outright in the UK.

However, any sense of closure about events at Armley would prove illusory. Asbestos is a remarkably enduring mineral; so are its adverse health effects. Mesothelioma deaths in the UK have continued to mushroom. In 2016, 2,595 individuals died of mesothelioma (in the late 1990s that figure was about 1,500 a year).[65] The J. W. Roberts' factory, which contaminated its workers, spewed asbestos into the surrounding streets, and spread the dust world-wide in its sprayed products has become a paradigm of the asbestos disaster. At the heart of that disaster is the kind of secondary or environmental exposures suffered by June Hancock and her neighbours at Armley. The latest government mesothelioma statistics show a frightening incidence of mesothelioma amongst building workers (in some mesothelioma cohorts nearly 50 per cent of the cases involve the building trades). The mesothelioma rate among women has also risen, with the increased risk apparently due to the widespread use of asbestos in buildings (such as schools).

By 2001, Leeds council had spent £4.5m decontaminating houses near the Roberts' factory at Armley, partly to encourage banks and building societies to start lending again for mortgages. In the UK, almost half of buildings constructed before 1999 are suspected of containing asbestos in various forms (that includes Roberts' Limpet asbestos).[66] Since

2000, therefore, the government has been forced to update its Control of Asbestos Regulations to combat exposure to decaying asbestos materials, to license their removal, and impose on property owners a duty to manage 'asbestos in place'. Private domestic properties are still currently exempt, however.

Compensation for asbestos-related diseases is as fraught as ever, despite June Hancock's fortitude in challenging T&N. At that time, the company had accepted liability for a further sixty claims from Armley and personal-injury lawyers had many more cases they hoped to settle. A year after that legal case (1996), T&N was sold to Federal Mogul, an American automotive parts manufacturer based in Michigan. The deal was masterminded by T&N chairman Sir Colin Hope, who had been responsible for the company doggedly obstructing the Hancock claim and misleading the courts about T&N's relationship with J. W. Roberts. T&N had a viable engineering division, but was burdened by asbestos liabilities, so it was puzzling why Federal Mogul had bought it. Its plans became clearer in 2001 when Federal Mogul filed for bankruptcy under Chapter 11. This legal haven allows American companies to ring-fence liabilities, whilst continuing to trade. Federal Mogul was still a profitable Fortune 500 company, but T&N's compensation payments ceased. Complicated wrangling then ensued about the extent of T&N's insurance coverage and how much money should be paid to T&N plaintiffs after Federal Mogul emerged from Chapter 11. Lawyers and campaigners representing Armley asbestos victims had little influence on the legal machinations in Michigan. Nor could they do anything to prevent the UK administrators and solicitors appointed by the bankruptcy courts racking up costs of £70m.

Nevertheless, UK lawyers continued to press the claims of fifty surviving Armley mesothelioma cases for which T&N had accepted liability. Belatedly in 2004, they were offered 24p in the £ in settlement of these claims.[67] To put that another way, T&N previously had paid an average of £100,000 per successful mesothelioma claim. Under the Federal Mogul–inspired deal, plaintiffs would receive (after deductions due to various costs) not much more than £20,000. Mesothelioma is a pitiless disease, which can kill in less than a year. Not surprisingly, all the claimants were dead by the time these payments were agreed. In 2007, after Federal Mogul had emerged fully from Chapter 11, the T&N Asbestos Trust was created in the UK. This deals with all claims made against T&N and its subsidiaries (including J. W. Roberts) with money set aside by the American parent. By 2008, no payments had been made by the

Trust; later payments for successful plaintiffs were only a small portion of the true value of such claims.

T&N's asbestos liabilities had, in effect, been taken offshore. Bankruptcy strategies, the offshoring of claims, and the exploitation of limited liability law (the 'corporate veil') have been characteristic responses by asbestos companies as they have attempted to escape liability and defend the continued production of asbestos.[68] These strategies underline the conclusion of my original article: that corporations, at worst, are about the manipulation of international law, unethical dealing, and the neglect of occupational and environmental health. The consequences can be seen in the catastrophic trend of asbestos cancer cases, which has still not peaked in the UK.

Notes

1 A. F. McEvoy, 'Working Environments: An Ecological Approach to Industrial Health and Safety', *Technology and Culture* 36 (Apr. 1995), S145–73. See also A. McIvor, 'Health and Safety in the Cotton Industry: A Literature Review', *Manchester Region History Review* 9 (1995), 50–7.
2 The most important action was Chase Manhattan Bank's $185 million damages suit against T&N for the removal of sprayed-asbestos from its New York skyscraper: *Chase Manhattan Bank v. T&N (87 Civ. 4436, Judge J. G. Koeltl), US District Court, Southern District of New York, 27 Oct.–6 Dec. 1995*. This article is based on Chase's microfilm copy of the T&N archive and uses the Bank's reel/frame numbers.
3 222/199. 'A History of J. W. Roberts Ltd up to 1964', typescript by A. N. M. [A. N. Marshall] and I. H. W.
4 *Turner & Newall Ltd: The First Fifty Years 1920–1970* (1970).
5 37/1487. 'General Administrative Regulations for the Unit Companies within the Group in the UK' (July 1939; reprinted July 1947).
6 A. C. Roberts was on the T&N board until 1924, when he retired to invest in the stock market and indulge his passion for horse-racing. W. N. Roberts joined the T&N board in 1928.
7 Chief Inspector of Factories and Workshops, *Annual Report . . . for the Year 1898* (London, 1899), Pt. II, p. 171. See also Morris Greenberg, 'Knowledge of the Health Hazard of Asbestos Prior to the Merewether and Price Report of 1930', *Social History of Medicine* 7 (Dec. 1994), pp. 493–516.
8 The worker involved was Nellie Kershaw, a TBA rover who had died in 1924 from 'asbestos poisoning'. See I. Selikoff and M. Greenberg, 'A Landmark Case in Asbestosis', *Journal of the American Medical Association* 265 (20 Feb. 1991), pp. 898–90.
9 See I. M. D. Grieve, 'Asbestosis' (Edinburgh University MD thesis, 1927), p. 1.
10 E. Margereson and June Hancock *v*. J. W. Roberts and T&N, High Court Leeds, before Mr. Justice Holland, June-October 1995. Trial transcript.

11 A. C. Haddow, 'Clinical Aspects of Pulmonary Fibrosis', *British Medical Journal* (28 Sept. 1929), pp. 580–1; Sir Thomas Oliver, 'Pulmonary Asbestosis in Clinical Aspects', *Journal of Industrial Hygiene* 9 (1927), pp. 483–5.

12 M. Greenberg, 'Professor Matthew Stewart: Asbestosis Research 1929–1934', *American Journal of Industrial Medicine* 32 (1997), pp. 562–9.

13 The 1969 Regulations set 2 fibres per cubic centimetre as a relatively safe limit.

14 Amosite, imported from South Africa (hence the acronym Asbestos Mines of South Africa), was the other main asbestos fibre. Like crocidolite, it had exceptional heat resistance and was used increasingly in Roberts' spray materials after the 1950s. This was despite the fact that amosite had long been banned as a raw material at TBA in Rochdale, because of its tendency to produce lethal dust. See 49/1564–5. W. J. Ellison to John Waddell, 10 Jan. 1968.

15 See N. J. Wikeley, 'Measurement of Asbestos Dust Levels in British Asbestos Factories in the 1930s', *American Journal of Industrial Medicine* 24 (1993), pp. 509–20.

16 43/290. Asbestosis Committee Minute Book, 8 Apr. 1932.

17 Brotherton Library, Leeds University, M. J. Stewart's Dairy, entry 22 Apr. 1929.

18 9/496–509. Bateman-Turner Report, Aug. 1932.

19 10/2086. W. N. Roberts to R. H. Turner, 15 July 1931.

20 W. N. Roberts' memo to Mr Shires, 10 July 1931.

21 Margereson/Hancock, trial transcript: Judgement, p. 23.

22 Evidence of Elmars Knabe, Margereson/Hancock transcript, pp. 79–94.

23 114/775. Engineers' report in Frederick A. Bentley *v.* J. W. Roberts, 16 Feb. 1979. Bentley, who worked at Roberts between 1951 and 1956, was awarded £18,000 and an admission that working conditions were far from ideal.

24 114/647–50. Testimony of Arthur E. Biddle (1921–73), who later died from asbestosis.

25 Evidence of William Parker, 'Margereson/Hancock' transcript, 27 June 1995, p. 3.

26 82/109–10. A. R. Milnes to A. N. Marshall, 6 Oct. 1971.

27 9/1540. Chapman & Co to J. L. Collins, 31 Oct. 1951. Original emphasis.

28 B. I. Castleman, *Asbestos; Medical and Legal Aspects* (Englewood Cliffs, NJ, 1996), pp. 300–11.

29 G. Tweedale and P. Hansen, 'Protecting the Workers: The Medical Board and the Asbestos Industry, 1930s to the 1960s', *Medical History* 42 (1998), pp. 439–57.

30 The Roberts' compensation case files as microfilmed by Chase Manhattan Bank seem to be the copies sent by Roberts to TBA.

31 The reasons are that death certificates do not always accurately record the cause of death; not all cases are reported to the coroner; and not all cases that are reported result in an inquest. See L. Arblaster et al, 'Asbestos Disease and Ccompensation', *British Medical Journal* 301 (10 Nov. 1990), p. 1101. Arblaster found that of 180 mesothelioma deaths in Leeds between 1971 and 1987, only 121 were the subject of an inquest; and only 154 had mesothelioma on the death certificate.

32 The links between asbestos and other cancers, such as those of the throat and gastro-intestinal tract, are still debated. Interestingly, both W. N. Roberts and

Norman Dolbey died of cancer: Roberts had cancer of the rectum; Dolbey had cancer of the prostate.

33 Brotherton Library, Leeds University, M. J. Stewart Diary, entry 4 June 1945.

34 Brotherton Library, Leeds University, M. J. Stewart Dairy, entry 30 March 1949 on Frederick Fallowes.

35 P. Bartrip, 'The Rise and Decline of Workmen's Compensation,' in P. Weindling (ed.), *The Social History of Occupational Health* (London, 1985), pp. 157–79.

36 Birch died after a stomach operation, with asbestosis as the major complicating factor.

37 In 1943, however, the basic figure was raised to £400.

38 Mesothelioma became a prescribed disease in 1966; lung cancer (in conjunction with asbestosis) only in 1985.

39 37/2139. J. L. Collins to Roberts, 10 Apr. 1945.

40 115/2131. TAC Construction Materials Ltd to Hepworth & Chadwick, 16 June 1972.

41 82/132. W. P. Howard to J. K. Roberts, Trafford Park, 14 Nov. 1974.

42 230/302–3. Leeds Director of Environmental Health to TAC Construction Materials Ltd, 3 Feb. 1978.

43 Asbestos Pollution and Mesothelioma', *Hansard*, 25 Nov. 1988.

44 Yorkshire TV, 'Too Close to Home', 6 Dec. 1988.500/523.

45 BBC TV, 'Deadly Legacy', 14 Apr. 1993.

46 Jenny Steele and Nick Wikeley, 'Dust on the Streets and Liability for Environmental Cancers', *Modern Law Review* 60 (1997), pp. 265–76.

47 Margereson/Hancock, Judgement, p. 39.

48 L. Arblaster, P. Hatton, D. Howel, E. Renvoize, M. Schweiger and L. M. Swinburne, 'Occupational and Environmental Links to Mesothelioma Deaths Occurring in Leeds during 1971 and 1987,' *Journal of Public Health Medicine* 17 (1995), pp. 297–304.

49 82/109–10. A. R. Milnes to A. N. Marshall, 6 Oct. 1971.

50 Ministry of Labour and Factory Inspectorate, *Annual Report . . . for 1956* (London, 1957), pp. 141–5.

51 Alan Marre, 'Report . . . to Max Madden MP . . . into a complaint made by J. P. Buick,' Mar. 1976.

52 In 1954, this time period was reduced to three years. Not until the 1960s was this law scrapped, so that plaintiffs could start proceedings within a year of their first knowledge of the injury.

53 Evidence of Eliza Shaw, Margereson/Hancock trial transcript, 28 June 1995, p. 21.

54 'History of Roberts', p. 34. This unpublished history makes no mention of asbestos disease, apart from a passing reference to the success of damping techniques with the spray process.

55 Grieve, 'Asbestosis', p. 13.

56 230/332–3. A. R. Milnes to J. D. Pennington, 8 June 1977.

57 In the 1950s, Turner & Newall's rate of profit (as a percentage of capital employed) was about 30 per cent, at a time when the rate for UK manufacturing industry was about 18 per cent.

58 110/161. D. J. Gates, 'Report on Training', 24 Aug. 1956. Gates observed that during bagging: 'the bag is filled to the approximate weight (which is

guessed at by the filler) in the bagging unit and then carried over to a pair of scales where the weight is adjusted either by taking away or adding fibre. After having the top sewn up, the bag is placed on the floor and jumped on several times to force it into the correct shape.' Gates also commented on the dustiness of the spray process.

59 2/1355–80. 'TBA and JWR: Rorganisation of Textile Manufacture', 31 Oct. 1949.

60 230/7–10. C. F. N. Hope to L. Arblaster, 25 Oct. 1989.

61 Interview with John Pickering, 8 Sept. 1997.

62 Margereson/Hancock trial transcript: Judgement, p. 5.

63 M. Punch, *Dirty Business: Exploring Corporate Misconduct* (London, 1996).

64 Barry Castleman and Geoffrey Tweedale, 'Turning the Tide: The Struggle for Compensation for Asbestos-Related Diseases and the Banning of Asbestos', in J. Melling and C. Sellers (eds.), *Dangerous Trade* (Philadelphia, PA, 2012), pp. 181–94.

65 Health & Safety Executive, *Mesothelioma in Great Britain 1968–2016.* Accessed 18 March 2109 at: www.hse.gov.uk/statistics/

66 Geoffrey Tweedale, 'Sprayed "Limpet" Asbestos: Technical, Commercial, and Regulatory Aspects', in G. Peters and B. J. Peters (eds.), *Sourcebook on Asbestos Diseases Vol. 20* (Charlottesville, VA, 1999), pp. 79–109.

67 'Leeds Asbestos' Victims New Payout', *Yorkshire Evening Post*, 8 October 2010.

68 Jock McCulloch and Geoffrey Tweedale, *Defending the Indefensible: The Global Asbestos Industry and Its Fight for Survival* (Oxford, 2008).

Chapter 3

The proprietorial theory of the firm and its consequences*

John Quail

Introduction

Business history has not noticeably concerned itself with questions of ideology.[1] The discipline generally studies business from the standpoint of what was done and how it was done. While business history has been used as grist to the mill of economic theory[2] the assumptions made by businessmen and managers of the past on the way a business could or should be run have not really been considered. In fact, UK business history has until recently been almost notoriously empiricist and untheoretical.[3] Furthermore, the study of the theoretical constructions of the past presents certain difficulties. Assumptions about the way business could or should be run are rarely spelled out as explicit finished systems of ideas but are implicit in conventions of thought and behaviour. While they are operative they do not have to be spelled out precisely because they are conventional. Nevertheless, drawing out the conventions of the past into an explicit theory of social action is well worth the effort. Such theories can explain much that otherwise appears bafflingly dysfunctional. Habits of thought, particularly when they are linked to economic interest can be long-lasting and influential and can have social effects long after the social conditions that gave rise to them have disappeared.

We are particularly concerned here with the late Nineteenth Century/ early Twentieth Century joint stock company in the UK. In the Western world the joint stock form provided the financial and organisational framework which allowed the growth of large firms. There were national variations in the way joint stock companies were organised, however, which had consequences for the way in which large enterprise could grow and adapt to changing circumstances. These companies, while subject to market forces, had escaped the institutional restrictions of a market co-ordinated economy.[4] The particular forms of organisation that the UK joint stock companies adopted therefore were not the result of localised institutional forces which dictated how they would do business but chosen because they were generally considered the right and prudent thing to do. These organisational forms, as we shall see, owed much to a set of principles based on the rights of property that persisted long after they had any basis in reality. More specifically they emphasised the particular roles and powers of joint stock company directors in a way which was to have significant consequences for the development of large UK business. These organisational principles we have called 'the proprietorial theory of the firm'.[5]

At the level of the firm the consequences of this theory are to be found in firm structure and control methods and the orchestration of professional/technical skills. Organised around the central principle of property rights, firms were seen as sets of operations carried out by employees supervised by representatives of the shareholders – the directors. In consequence there was a perceived clear separation of roles between proprietors and managers analogous to the separation of politicians and civil servants. In other developed economies it seems to have been far easier for boards of directors to have evolved from committees of owners into the highest tier of management. The particular emphasis on the separate role and prerogatives of the directors in the UK led to a fixity of structure which had two broad consequences at the level of the firm. Firstly firms did not evolve managerial hierarchies much beyond the departmental or functional level, top management being sparse or non-existent with management technique consequently being generally under-developed. Secondly firms could not easily grow beyond a certain size or complexity of operation or respond dynamically to changing business conditions. At the level of the UK economy as a whole the proprietorial theory of the firm was a key ideological contribution to the intractability of UK business in the face of a desperate need for adaptability and change in the inter-war years and beyond. As such it should be considered an important component of the UK's relative economic decline in the Twentieth Century.

The prorietorial theory of the firm

There was no convenient contemporary explicit summary of the system of ideas behind the organisation of the late Nineteenth Century/early Twentieth Century UK joint stock company. This should not be taken to imply that there was no such system or that any such system was not coherent. In order to demonstrate a coherent whole, however, it is necessary to gather together partial expressions of an implicit system of ideas from a number of sources. Statute and case law gave particular emphasis and clarity to certain aspects of what was considered the 'right' way to run a company. Business and legal journals commented on changes in the law, for example the first recognition of managing directors in the 1908 Companies Act. Practical handbooks for accountants and others give explanations of company structure and business practice from their own partial viewpoint. The picture that emerges from these different sources shows considerable consistency.

The governing body of a joint stock company is a board of directors. Under the Companies Acts 'management is almost always entrusted by the Articles [of Association] to the directors and *they exercise all the powers* for the conduct of the business possessed by the company'[6] (my italics). Directors' duties are not laid down in detail in company law but depend on the specific Articles of Association of the company, a general requirement to act with honesty and 'some degree of both skill and diligence'[7] appropriate to the circumstances, and also the way in which it is agreed that tasks are to be distributed between directors and employees. Directors have a duty of trust to the shareholders to whom they must account for their stewardship 'as commercial men managing a trading concern for the benefit of themselves and of all the other shareholders in it'.[8] The powers of directors were thus very great while their responsibilities were rather imprecise.

The early assumption was that the large powers given to the directors would be balanced by the democratic rights of the shareholders as a whole exercised in general meetings. In reality, however, the exercise of these powers was undermined by changes in the nature both of shareholdings and shareholders.[9] From the 1880s onwards there was a tendency towards holdings of a decreasing individual size in any company in the hands of an increasing number of shareholders. There was an increasing tendency among investors towards the actuarial approach of portfolio building which intrinsically tended away from attempts at active influence. Shareholder attendance at general meetings declined. As a result of these tendencies, control by the directors of a joint stock company that was already strong became stronger as they increasingly became self-perpetuating oligarchies. Despite this decreasing shareholder control and increasing directorial autonomy, the theoretical justification for the large powers of boards of directors remained their role as a group of proprietors standing for the proprietors as a whole. This had a number of consequences for the way in which the job of director was perceived and carried out.

As shareholders' representatives directors were expected to be significant financial stakeholders. In this respect practice was more insistent that the law. The Companies Acts required no share qualification in 1862 and from 1906 asked only that a director hold 'at least one share in the company' but it was normal practice to make appointments as a director conditional on substantial qualifying shareholdings. *The Stock Exchange Year Book* for 1908 shows shareholding qualification for directors of the top 50 companies to be between £1,000 and £4,000 for railways, £1,000 and £8,000 for industrial companies and £5,000 and £10,000 for banks. (The 1993 equivalent of £1,000 in 1908 is £21,000.) It was current expert opinion that 'one of the main elements of success' of a public company was 'the presence upon the directorate, and the management, of men holding a substantial interest in the ordinary or unprotected stocks.'[10] In 1902, giving an indication of what a 'substantial interest' might be, a prominent company promoter was of the opinion that on flotation the owner-managers should hold at least one third of the equity to demonstrate that it was a going concern.[11] J. B. Jefferys quotes the *Economist* as urging shareholders to test the soundness of their investment by examining the share registers of their company to check that their directors were not selling shares.[12]

But if directors were expected to be stakeholders they were not expected to be experts. This was a complaint of nineteenth century railway shareholders: 'As one disgruntled London and North Western shareholder put it: "in the vast majority of cases they [railway directors] are elected for every other reason than because they have expert knowledge of railway business." This was true.'[13] The *Economist* wrote in 1912: '. . . there is still a feeling that directorships call for no particular skill or knowledge and that anyone with a reasonable amount of application may fill a seat at a board with credit and responsibility.'[14] The *Accountant* stated in 1930: 'directors of great commercial undertakings . . . need have no qualifications save the ability to subscribe for the requisite number of shares as provided in the company's articles of association . . .'[15] Indeed, there was even apparently hostility to the idea that experts be appointed to the board at all, as demonstrated by the statement of the Parliamentary Secretary of the Board of Trade in 1915:

> the opinion of businessmen . . . is that if you have an expert or two experts on a board of directors they practically command the situation . . . and a number of businessmen prefer on that account to be able to take their counsel without having their counsellor a co-director when he would be practically in a position to give orders.[16]

The board of directors exercised its authority as a collective body at intermittent meetings. Directors were not expected (nor did they expect) to take any individual responsibility for management of parts of the business. Case law established that an individual director 'is not bound to give continuous attention to the affairs of his company'.[17] The consequence was that the role of director qua director was part-time. Prior to 1908 the implied legal disapproval of directors taking 'any other office or place of profit'[18] in the company was apparently taken seriously: the articles 'usually renders the office [of Director] vacant' under these circumstances according to a contemporary guide.[19] The law thus permitted and even encouraged a situation where boards were composed of people giving the minimum of time and attention that the law required. This minimum was not onerous. As one disenchanted manager of a steel works put it in 1879: 'the higher management of great works . . . as a rule is not as it should be . . . for some unaccountable reason it seems to have become the opinion that gentlemen without special training, often engaged in other business of an entirely different sort, and coming only occasionally to the works as directors, can adequately and efficiently control and manage great manufactures.'[20]

Directors, then, were not expected to be full time, expert or exert close supervision. But if this was the case, who was to run the business? It was inevitable that tasks had to be delegated to full-time managers and there was nothing in law to stop this. A director was safe from the law if he could demonstrate that the delegation of tasks was 'reasonable . . . in the circumstances, and . . . not inconsistent with any express provisions of the Articles of Association.'[21] The oversight of such delegated tasks by directors was expected to be carried out with reasonable care compatible with the skills of the director but the honesty of managers could be assumed unless there was evidence to the contrary. Case law held that directors were not required to check the correctness of information given them by managers unless there were grounds for suspicion.[22] The law was at its most emphatic where oversight of payments was concerned[23] but no continuous oversight of managers was required, supervision being carried out by the intermittent meetings of the board or its properly constituted committees.

There was no reason in law therefore why delegations to management should not have been extensive. The praxis of the period, however, was generally considerably more restrictive. This was the direct result of a perceived sharp separation between the respective roles of directors and managers:

> The constitution of a joint stock company is democratic and is composed of the shareholders who elect the administrative [i.e. the

directors] who elect (sic) and supervise the executive [i.e. the managers]. If the latter two are mixed up there is no protection for the former and it is most essential that the distinction between administrative and executive should be jealously guarded.[24]

The directors were to establish general policy and the managers were to carry it out. As the *Economist* put it in 1912:

the common theory of a director is that he acts more or less like the head of a Government Department bringing a sound general knowledge of business to the conduct of a particular concern, taking the advice of permanent officials but deciding broad questions of policy for himself.[25]

Even for the post World War One advocate of scientific management, Lyndall Urwick, the separation of the duties of directors and managers along these lines was crucial:

. . . it is of particular importance to define the activities which properly belong to a Board of Directors and those which form part of the duty of a Manager and are concerned with the executive control of the enterprise. One definition which has been suggested reads: '*Administration* is the function of industry concerned with the determination of the corporate policy, co-ordination of production, finance and distribution, the settlement of the compass of the organisation and the ultimate control of the executive.' Over against this are set the duties of management. '*Management* is the function of industry concerned with the carrying out of policy within the limits set up by administration and the employment of the organisation for the particular objects set before it.'[26]

These definitions make it clear that boards of directors, generally meeting monthly, were not only supposed to set the general policy which managers were expected to implement but to co-ordinate the various functions of the organisation. Yet the theoretical separation of policy and execution had to coexist with the practicalities of running a business which required responses to events on a daily if not hourly basis. Delegation and co-ordination to an extent necessary to achieve commercial success could clearly be in tension with the part-time directors desire to keep control.

One practical solution for the board was to appoint one or more of their number as managing directors with more frequent attendance and delegated powers. Managing directors had become established by the time of the large-scale amalgamations of the late nineteenth century but they had no mention in statute until the Companies Act of 1908. By delegating power to one of their own the directors kept power within the board. In so doing, however, they raised immediate problems over confusion of function and an apparent breach of the principle of directors' collective responsibility. Giving the power to run a joint stock business to an individual was seen as dubious if not dangerous.[27] L. R. Dicksee, Professor of Accounting at the LSE, felt able to say in a text-book for his students published in 1910:

> ... cases are by no means unknown in which very large powers have been vested in the Managing Director, but as a rule with no great measure of success. So far as this country is concerned, at all events, the cases in which the all-powerful Managing Director comes most to the front are when the company has failed under such circumstances as to involve a somewhat protracted enquiry on the part of the Official Receiver. Possibly for that reason we are inclined to look askance at anything approaching plenary powers being granted to any one individual.[28]

If delegations to managing directors were constrained this applied *a fortiori* to general managers who were not directors. As a result of the constraints placed on the managing director and the wide powers assumed by the board the scope allowed to salaried managers was narrow. The management writer John Lee compared UK and US practice in 1922. In the US, he says, both administrative and executive tasks are undertaken by the president and his general managers. However in the UK

> where there is a differentiation between administrative and executive, the line [between policy and execution] is often drawn rather lower down than in America: that is to say, the manager becomes an immediate works manager rather than a principal executive officer, so that a managing director . . . undertakes more executive functions than his American prototype. In some cases this is certainly overdone. That is to say the chief direction does not content itself with judging by managerial statistics or by summed results and afterwards with allowing the chief executive a considerable range of liberty of action, but he discusses questions of individual remuneration and of methods of work in detail in a way which must rob the

executive of some authority and, indeed of some dignity, and what is more to be regretted, of some responsibility.[29]

Sometimes, indeed, it appears that the managing director, who might attend more regularly but like his fellow-directors could still be part time, dispensed with a chief of the executive altogether. In 1929, Urwick, while claiming that the practice was in decline, pointed to a significant proportion of businesses 'which lack a full time managing director or general manager' resulting in factories

> with sales manager, production manager, labour manager, chief technical engineer, finance manager, and education officer, all working quite separately and happily at their own specific tasks, without any executive co-ordination whatever by a general manager. There are, indeed, many factories in Great Britain attempting to work along these extraordinary lines, usually because the managing director is so incapable of delegating authority, and so busy with other preoccupations, that he imagines that the necessary co-ordination of the efforts of his various subordinates can be achieved at a weekly board meeting . . .[30]

It was not the incapacity of the individual managing director which causes the lack of delegation, however, but a general theory and practice of the firm that discouraged delegation and accepted intermittent attendance by directors.

Our discussion of UK corporate governance may be summarised as follows: the organisational principles which determined the structures of UK joint stock companies centralised power in a board of directors who were expected to be stakeholders but did not need to be expert or exert close or continuous supervision of managers. Delegations to managers were inevitable yet directors nervous of their liabilities and prerogatives were unwilling to delegate beyond the minimum. As we shall see the consequence was that boards would create directors committees rather than delegate to managers. Single chief executive officers could be appointed from time to time but for the most part either temporarily or under constraints which made wider delegations to managers minimal. We shall also see that though the capacity of the board to manage and co-ordinate the firm was limited by time spent on the task or possibly through lack of expertise, the grip of the board on the organisation was firm in its power to block initiatives or spending or to limit the power of managers to make decisions. We shall furthermore also see that as a result of the reservation of the co-ordinating role to the board the development of top management was limited, organisation of the firm tended to be narrowly departmental and the roles of employed professionals were kept narrow in scope. The consequence was a meagre output of managerial human capital.

Consequences: firm structure

We shall now look at the structures actually adopted by the 50 largest companies in the UK before World War One. The firms examined are taken from the lists compiled by Peter Wardley and others.[31] A further list of firms in order of capitalisation is shown in the section Appendix: large companies in 1905. These lists demonstrate that by far the biggest category of large firm was the railway company: railways are the ten largest companies; they make up 15 of the top 20 and between half and two thirds of the top fifty, depending on the criteria used. Measures of size by market value give a group of about ten banks. The balance of the top 50 largest firms are manufacturing firms, most of which are amalgamations. We shall take these categories in order.

Railways

Like other early nineteenth century joint stock companies[32] the new railway companies assumed that it was the job of the directors to manage the company directly:

> In 1831 the Directors of the Liverpool and Manchester railway were solemnly deliberating such matters as the bad loading of an individual wagon, the dismissal of a clerk for drunkenness . . . in short, endeavouring to conduct the day by day management of the line.[33]

This soon became impossible and the directors had to delegate tasks to paid officials but reserved as much power as they could to themselves. The consequence was that as functional officers were appointed as functions were split (for example by separating responsibilities for locomotive and carriage & wagon building) or increased (for example by ferry operation or hotels) committees of directors were set up to supervise each of the functions. Chief functional officers were generally appointed *but no chief executive officer*. As an American observer put it: All the main functional officers 'were co-ordinate, and nobody short of the directorate, unskilled in railroad operation could harmonise their work on the interests of the whole company'.[34] That is to say all the chief officers were equal in status and independent. Only the board, acting through committees, had the power to tell chief officers what to do. The Chairman of the Railway Shareholders Association contrasted the situation in the UK with US railroads where

> Vice Presidents [are] in charge of special departments – finance, stores, etc. Presumably their place is occupied [in the UK] by the Committees of Directors who do a large amount of departmental supervision. These may not be so expert as their American counterparts, and they may not have such a firm hold on all the administrative details, but on the other hand they are in much closer touch with the shareholders.[35]

The number of committees of the board could be large, with the various internal supervisory committees supplemented by joint committees with other railways. The sheer numbers of committees must raise questions as to the effectiveness of the system. In 1907 the relatively modest North Eastern Railway had between six and seven functional supervisory committees.[36] The Midland Railway had ten to twelve supervisory committees and anywhere between 16 and 27 joint or representative committees.[37] The London and North Western Railway (LNWR) had fully 16 supervisory committees and 39 joint or representative committees.[38]

The directors, furthermore, spent limited time on the task of supervising railway companies. Board committees and the board itself generally met monthly. On the LNWR, for example, there was a strict timetable of meetings compressed into two days. Functional/departmental committees with slots of one or one and a half hours were run in parallel on the first day with the Finance Committee and full Board meeting on the second day.[39] On the evidence of the records of those meetings, the business conducted was overwhelmingly routine with a great emphasis on approving expenditure items down to tiny sums: lists of "debts and defalcations", approvals for repairs to fences, lists of all approved wage rises in all departments fill the books. These expenditures were in turn approved by the Board.[40]

Inevitably the question must arise of where the power lay in such an apparently thinly controlled system. It could be argued that such a system allowed sufficient freedom to managers to innovate. This is to ignore the key element in the power relationship between board and officers: managers might propose but the directors disposed. In a number of key ways the directors retained control: they controlled expenditure, they determined the management structure and in consequence they controlled the careers and aspirations of managers. Managers' careers were overwhelmingly limited to single 'watertight' departments[41] and the heavily regulated and rule-run nature of the work limited aspirations. The board's function was a static form of supervision rather than innovation and organisational change and boards were able to resist proposals for change from managers without effort. The board and management structures of railways were in consequence rigid and long-lasting.

Banking

British banking was transformed between the late 1870s and the four years after World War One when a 'final frenzy' produced the 'Big Five'.[42] Stimulated by slump and a banking crisis in 1878 to diversify and increase deposits to reduce risk, expanding banks began to acquire others in mergers of ever-increasing size. As a smaller number of ever-larger competitors emerged their ambitions crystallised into the achievement of a national branch network and, where they were a country bank, to acquire a London base to carry out the lucrative trade of the City.

The governance of banks varied according to the degree to which autonomy was retained by the constituent firms making up an amalgamation. Three banks may be taken to represent the range of variation: the Midland, Barclays and Lloyds. The Midland was the most ruthless in suppressing the identity of acquired banks. The result was a business run from its London HQ with barely a trace of local autonomy.[43] Barclays stood at the other extreme. It was formed in 1896 in a defensive merger by 20 private banks who wanted the safety of size without the loss of local autonomy. Barclays had a board of directors and an HQ in London but the individual amalgamating banks became 'Local Head Offices' and their former partners became local directors. As Barclays expanded by further acquisitions it distributed branch banks among existing Local Head Offices or created new ones. By 1926 there were 33 local head offices.[44] Lloyds Bank took a middle course between these extremes: the boards of the more prominent acquired banks continued as local committees whose influence, however important initially, was allowed to steadily decline over subsequent decades.[45]

The key commercial decisions that banks had to make were decisions on loans. The limits to which branches could lend without reference to directors were relatively low: the Midland required board decisions on loans over £2,000 but others had limits as low as £300.[46] As a result the volume of work that directors reserved to themselves was large and committees of directors had to be formed and meet frequently to cover it. Generally it was said that boards met weekly and held board committee meetings on three or four days a week.[47] This is confirmed by arrangements at the Midland: by 1900 it had five board committees and they and the board met weekly. (The process was to continue, six more board committees would be added by the 1930s.)[48] Barclays and Lloyds varied from this pattern only to the extent that these decisions were delegated geographically to local directors' committees rather than committees of the main board meeting centrally.

Because the commercial decision-making was largely reserved to the board and its committees the role of senior management was restricted to control of the administrative structure. At the top of the management structure the Midland, Lloyds and Barclays all had single chief executive officers as long as they were going through their dynamic periods of amalgamation and expansion. Edward Holden of the Midland also extraordinarily combined his chief executive function as managing director (from 1898) with that of Chairman (from 1908) until his death in 1919. The Midland's last major merger was in 1918. Barclays kept a single general manager until a last major merger in 1918. At Lloyds a single general manager was in place until his retirement at the end of a series of three post-World War One take-overs between 1918 and 1923.

Once this period of expansion ended, however, these banks did not keep single chief executives but relied instead on joint general managers. The Midland used its three existing ones. Barclays added a further three to its existing one. Lloyds appointed five, later reduced to three. The effect of these appointments was to emphasise the co-ordinating role of the board and its committees and to remove any empowered co-ordination below the level of the board. Thus as banks moved from what might be called the heroic to the organised phase, the boards moved to decisively weaken managerial power. It has to be said, however, that the consequence was no obvious weakening of operational control or commercial effectiveness. This may be because the business of branch banking was a simple one, the methods of controlling operations were well established and the comfortable oligarchic position of the banks did not bring strong competitive pressure to bear.

Amalgamated manufacturing firms

There was a wide variation in the extent to which the large amalgamated firms formed in the late Nineteenth and early Twentieth Century were integrated. Some were little more than aggregations of the private partnerships that had existed prior to merger and flotation. The large breweries were of this type as was Imperial Tobacco.[49] In these cases proprietorial power determined the structure of the firms absolutely. Other amalgamated firms, however, had to adapt and change to a greater or lesser extent because of their internal complexity and/or market pressures.

  Steel, Armaments, Shipbuilding Conglomerates (Vickers, Armstrong Whitworth.) These firms by various mergers, acquisitions or partial acquisitions constructed themselves as shipbuilders and armaments suppliers in the last decade of the nineteenth and the first decade of the twentieth century.[50] They were all multi-plant, multi-process companies within which one might have expected great returns from efficient control. But while *technical* advances were made such as the specification of armour plate, the firms remained too loosely integrated and controlled to realise their potential advantages. This looseness of control manifested itself both as between the separate sites and the centre and within the sites themselves. The companies could survive and prosper with this type of structure and control before World War I but were left dangerously exposed in the inter-war years.

  Vickers began its diversification out of steel in the 1880s. As it grew by acquisition the owners and managers of the acquired firms were left in place even when the subsidiary was wholly owned. Throughout its life Vickers was run by a single board of directors without standing committees. The board could and did exert strong control when events brought inefficient working or owner-manager intransigence forcibly to the board's attention. It is also clear, however, that there was inefficient working and unproductive local management wilfulness in a number of subsidiaries over a number of years. The board, then, did not manage its constituent parts in any detail, effectively delegating operations without corresponding return flows of management information or a centrally determined investment strategy. The fallibility of a structure controlled in this way was demonstrated by the uncontrolled diversification and collapse of the firm immediately after World War One.[51] They were, nevertheless, an admired, feared and profitable firm before the War.

  Armstrong Whitworth had acquired a range of facilities in steel, shipbuilding and armaments by 1900. Its profit record was less satisfactory than Vickers despite a more compact ownership structure.[52] The most likely cause of this poor performance was the dominance within the board of a small coterie led by Sir Andrew Noble and his sons. Noble, unlike the Vickers family, resisted the importation of new blood on to the board even when this was necessary to keep open commercial channels between the firm and its most important client, the UK government.

There was a short-lived attempt at change by a group on the board who forced a number of reforms between 1911 and 1913. One was the institution of local directors, that is single top managers in each of the constituent firms with quasi board powers who met in a 'local board' but who were not members of the board of directors itself. Other reforms were the formation of a finance committee of the board to increase financial control and new recruitment to the board. With the death of the leader of the reform group and the subsequent effects of the First World War 'the reforms . . . never really took root and the management structure of the company remained largely unaltered.'[53] As in the case of Vickers, Armstrong Whitworth were unable to adapt to the volatile trading conditions after World War One. The firm collapsed in 1927.

Textiles (J and P Coats, Fine Cotton Spinners, Bleachers Association, Calico Printers Association.) A wave of 18 amalgamations took place in the textile sector between 1896 and 1900. In large textile firms formed by amalgamation, the organisational structure and immediate effectiveness of the firm varied according to the number of amalgamating firms. The range was considerable: J and P Coats Ltd was formed from the acquisition by Coats of its three chief and most prosperous rivals in the production of sewing thread while the Calico Printers Association was formed from 59 constituent companies. Despite the obvious desire of some participants to achieve greater control of the market, all the firms involved faced strong competition. Their structures therefore had to be commercially effective.

The Coats board was dominated by Coats family members[54] though the firm was greatly influenced in its structure and management style by O. E. Philippi who had been foreign sales manager but had risen to a position equivalent to chief executive officer. In 'all except manufacturing operations he became the main focus of decision-making, and increasingly decisions about manufacturing came to respond to his suggestions and demands. Other directors, with the exception of the chairman . . . were very specialised in their individual departments.'[55] There appears to have been a 'flat' departmental structure with the home factories run by family or vendor directors/managers. Foreign factories were run by managers reporting to Philippi who also held the reins of all the sales organisations which reported to him personally. It is nevertheless necessary to stress that Philippi remained one board member among many. The board was not ornamental and there were directors' committees for General Purposes, Works, Finance and Development. Philippi could remain as influential as he was only so long as he retained the support of his board.

We may conclude therefore that J and P Coats may be best considered as an extremely well run personally managed firm before World War One. It relied on a working board and key individuals within it to manage the organisation directly, and the control systems it evolved were designed to serve that structure. It was highly vulnerable to the loss of those key individuals but meanwhile remained significantly more prosperous than its UK competitors, retaining market share and margins without suffering any apparent diseconomies of increased scale.

Generally speaking, the structure adopted by other textile amalgamations had to reconcile the apparently unquestioned principle that the management of the constituent factories remained in the hands of the ex-owners with the need for centrally organised consistency of practice and co-ordination. Since many of the amalgamations were a response to intense competition and the period also saw quite severe fluctuations in raw material prices, central control over buying and selling was essential. The allocation of production to individual factories, the concentration of production, the closing of inefficient plants and the gathering of cost data in a form which allowed such decisions to be made all clearly required a significant degree of central authority.[56]

Central co-ordination was more difficult to achieve the larger the number of firms amalgamating and the larger the size of the board of directors. The Fine Cotton Spinners and Doublers (FCSD) was an amalgamation of 29 firms, the Bleachers Association 53 and the Calico Printers Association (CPA) 59. Generally, each firm would be represented on the board of directors although vendors could be bought-out completely or some firms could have multiple representatives. The FCSD had a board of 26 directors, the Bleachers Association 49 and the CPA fully 84.

From the beginning the FCSD adopted the expedient of delegating many matters to an 'executive board' of seven meeting weekly co-ordinating the work of an unknown number of managing directors who were based centrally and whose job was to work directly with the vendor managers. But the vendor managers were also the directors of the amalgamation so they were being supervised by men they nominally controlled. It was Macrosty's opinion that the power in the organisation lay, on balance with the executive. But it was 'always a delicate situation and depends for its possibility entirely on the personal qualities of the men concerned.'[57] Even in the most successful amalgamation, then, the structure was as much the result of a shareholders democracy as of commercial imperatives.

The FCSD was also centrally co-ordinated through a central office composed of a statistical department 'which enables a close comparison . . .

of the concerns doing the same class of work.' There were also central departments for buying, selling, machinery and for 'the ordinary secretarial and accounts work.'[58] The central office, which was presumably under the day to day control of the managing directors also controlled selling prices.

The Bleachers Association initially had looser arrangements: the board delegated operational matters to two general managers while attempting to co-ordinate matters with 'mass meetings of forty-nine directors' as Macrosty puts it.[59] Things clearly got out of hand and in 1904 the board delegated powers to a smaller executive body and restricted the powers of the general managers. The result would appear to be a structure close to that of the FCSD. Nothing appears available on the functions and responsibilities of the Bleachers Association central office, thought there is circumstantial evidence that they were very similar to the FCSD.[60]

The CPA's early arrangements were similar to those of the Bleachers Association but on a larger scale – 84 directors co-ordinating 3 managing directors. Chaos ensued and the CPA were unable to resolve the matter internally. The directors and shareholders appointed a committee in 1902 to investigate and make proposals for re-organisation.[61] The investigatory committee declared its aim to be to make the CPA 'one concern consisting of a number of component parts, controlled by a central authority.' Interestingly the committee considered that one of the problems with the company had been that because of time pressures on the managing directors they were 'compelled . . . to depute much of their work to permanent officials. This knowledge could not but increase the resistance both active and passive, to instructions emanating from head office.' This resistance by vendor managers to non-proprietors' instructions is clearly felt to be not unreasonable. A key point in favour of the new scheme was that if it was not adopted the directors would still 'have to rely on the assistance of permanent officials appointed by themselves . . .' The scheme the committee proposed was a three tier system. At the top was a board of 6 directors of whom three were outside directors. There was then an executive of three (the managing directors) and finally seven advisory committees drawn from the managements of constituent firms to deal with technical and policy matters ranging from production and its concentration to raw materials and marketing. For all their concern with central authority the committee emphasised the need for the consent of the governed. While they roundly asserted that any refusal by vendor managers to carry out the executive's orders would be a sacking offence they stressed that 'it is of the greatest importance . . . that all instructions given by the Executive should be known to be the outcome of careful deliberation and of sound practical and up to date knowledge of the matters to which they refer. Unless this is the case such instructions would be carried our reluctantly.'

The advisory committees were the means whereby consensus could be achieved. However, despite their title they had more than advisory powers: 'it will be the duty of the Executive to carry the recommendations of the Advisory Committees into effect' said the Committee, though disputes between the executive and advisory committees could be adjudicated by the board. Executive members were to attend board meetings though they would have no vote and they were to share attendances at advisory committee meetings between them. The effect of this structure was to multiply the functions covered in detail by the board by creating seven executives, understanding that word in the sense it was used by the FCSD or the Bleachers Association, where those latter organisations had one. Just as in the case of the railways and the banks, the desire by owners of equity to keep control of matters in detail resulted in a system of committees.

Other large amalgamated firms for whom we have information also appear to lie within the spectrum of the organisational types we have seen above. Associated Portland Cement Manufacturers, formed by an amalgamation of 27 firms in 1900, had a large board of directors (33 in 1906) which met monthly. Fourteen managing directors met weekly and formed committees for finance and general purposes, works and sales.[62] Guest Keen and Nettlefold was formed in 1902 from three firms whose combination brought integration vertically from iron ore and coal mining through steel production to bolt and screw manufacture. A single board of directors was formed for the amalgamation but 'individual companies [were] allowed to continue functioning almost as autonomous units'[63] and before World War One each constituent firm retained its own offices. Co-ordination and matters of detail were delegated to five committees of directors.

Our brief survey of the structure of large UK joint stock companies in the late nineteenth and early twentieth century shows some common features. The ambition of the board was to control their businesses and the frontier of control between the board and management was set at a point which either by business structure (e.g. the railways) or reserved decisions (e.g. the banks) reduced the scope of management. The consequence was that some organisations, particularly the railways, could be both over-centralised and under-managed. Other amalgamated businesses could be more federal in structure where proprietorial interests persisted in constituent parts though the scope of management was not thereby increased. There is evidence that there was a tension between commercial imperatives which dictated delegation to management and the desire for board control. In the case of the banks when the commercial imperatives which had seen them appoint single chief executives disappeared they reasserted their power by appointing multiple general managers instead. There was no ratchet effect where an increase in managerial scope became irreversible.

Our survey shows that the directors of large companies formed committees of the board rather than delegate tasks to management when they felt unable to supervise the main elements of their business through the board alone. Sometimes these committees carried out specific functions like the banking committees making decisions on loans. In other cases committees would supervise senior officers, for example the departmental committees on the railways, or develop policy like the CPA advisory committees. In all these cases, however, the committees occupied the organisational space which would have otherwise required senior professional managers. We are given some clues as to why the managerial option was not chosen which are clearly rooted in the proprietorial theory of the firm. We can see from the CPA reorganisation that a non-proprietorial professional management structure giving orders to proprietor vendor managers was simply out of consideration. We can perhaps understand the status panic involved. It is significant, however, that elsewhere there was a preference for a proprietorial structure even when it was clear that the managerial option was more effective. This was the position taken by the Chairman of the Railway Shareholders Association: committees of directors might not be as expert as professional managers, he said, and they might not have such a firm grip of all the administrative details but they were in much closer touch with the shareholders. Influence was clearly preferable to effectiveness.

We can see from the survey of firm structure that top management was sparse or non-existent. This was the corollary of the perceived role of the board and its committees. Top management emerged in US and German big business in the later nineteenth and early twentieth century.[64] The function of top management is the evaluation, co-ordination and control of middle managers and the allocation of resources between constituent divisions or enterprises. They are also the source of collective corporate entrepreneurship. With the emergence of top management came a new intensity and depth of management, often experimental in attitude and technique and well beyond the minimum immediate requirements of the business. But it developed a depth of professional expertise which enabled US and German corporations to build larger and more complex organisations and co-ordinate them efficiently so that the market dominance which size brought was not undermined by dysfunctions of scale or complexity. It was this depth of expertise and the adaptability that came with it that was forgone by the large UK firm through its attachment to a system of supervision by a proprietorial board. We shall also see in the next section that the organisation of the large UK firm at departmental level tended to under-develop the potentially managerial technical and professional personnel at its disposal.

Consequences: human capital

If extensive professional management structures were to develop to integrate and co-ordinate new large-scale firms there were really only two groups of professionals who were part prepared for the role: engineers and accountants.[65] Both, in varying degrees, routinely managed men and processes and gathered numerical data as a means to that management. It is undoubtedly the case that in the UK both professions needed to add considerably to the scope of their work before they became full-blown Chandlerian managers but both possessed key component skills. The roles assigned to engineers and accountants within UK firms are important, therefore, because they demonstrate how competent the professionals were to take on any expanded role and how ready their employers were to let them do so.

The role of both the engineer and the accountant within the UK enterprise was narrow. We will take the engineer first. The training of the engineer was narrow in two senses. It was purely technical and based in systems of apprenticeship/pupillage. In the 1880s external training was opposed by employers on the grounds that trade secrets would be revealed.[66] The Civil and Mechanical Engineers were opposed to qualifying examination at this time, too.[67] These obstacles to a more broadly based training lifted only slowly. College studies slowly gained a higher profile. The mechanical engineers instituted their first qualifying examinations in 1913. But neither college education nor qualifying exams included any organisation, management or cost accounting matters.[68]

The apprentice/pupillage training of the engineer was circumscribed by the engineers role in production: 'In this country the opinion has prevailed that in [technically based] industries the problems which present themselves fall under two separable, distinct and independent heads viz. the "technical" and the "administrative" . . . engineers are supposed to deal especially with the former.' Every other 'financial, commercial or administrative problem' was outside the engineer's sphere.[69] It would appear that the engineer as such was excluded from many aspects of production such as labour hire and fire, job sequencing, progress control and quality control which were the foremen's responsibility. Rate-fixing and cost accounting were carried out by specialist clerks.[70] This left the engineer with the drawing board and the machines.

There was a natural career progression for the engineer into works management.[71] Engineers were not prepared for management by their training which did not include administrative matters or labour management: 'the art of managing men . . . is usually regarded . . . by Capital as a sort of customary by-product of technical ability', as one observer put it, to be learned, like engineering, on the job.[72] By the end of World War One it was clear that engineers were aware that professional narrowness had weakened their ability to manage.[73] The war had revealed a generally low level of management ability: an engineer whose war-time duties had taken him to many factories was to say

> . . . the weak spot throughout these factories has been the works management and the business side in general. It is painful sometimes to see how little ability the management has shown. I think one could hardly have found a direction in which our education is more lacking than in that of getting what is, after all, only common sense into our engineers.[74]

The explanation for the engineers' restricted role must lie with the tasks and expectations laid upon them by their employers. It is significant, for example, that engineers and indeed works management generally were excluded from access to cost data. Costs and cost systems were regarded by manufacturers as trade secrets.[75] A leader in an engineering magazine in 1893 spoke of the 'rigid precautions adopted by manufacturing engineers to confine all knowledge of the costs department to the staff of clerks engaged in the work [which] renders it impossible for the young engineer to learn anything of the system during his apprenticeship.'[76] A chemical engineer employed by the Ministry of Munitions wrote in 1918; 'until comparatively recently . . . it was customary at many plants to keep the chemists in complete ignorance not only of the costs at these plants but also even of the efficiencies.'[77] he separation of costing information from the managers of production was quite deliberate and contemporary books on management are explicit on the matter.[78] Sir Herbert Austin, speaking to the Cost and Works Accountants in 1920 made it clear that the cost accountant was the managing director's policeman as far as production was concerned.[79]

Before World War One engineers appear generally to have accepted their narrow role. Some may even have gloried in it. Commenting on his fellow engineers lack of commercial attitude, a local chairman of the electrical engineers said in 1917, 'It is more charitable to ourselves to say that engineers have been absorbed and engrossed by the "mechanical" interest in engineering to the neglect of its "business" requirements than to say that we have ignored and looked askance at anything so ordinary as commercialism . . .'[80] Another could say 'Thirty years ago I had a contemptuous feeling for anything connected with the commercial side of engineering . . .' and could describe a distinct general tendency to despise commercial work.[81] The existence of such attitudes could only reinforce and prolong the retardation of the process of turning engineers into managers.

If accountants were to become managers they too had to overcome the restrictions imposed by a narrow professional role. Accountancy as a profession grew as a result of insolvency work and the audit of company accounts.[82] Both these roles were external to the day to day running of the firm and were largely the consequence of legislation or shareholder anxiety rather than the organic demands of businesses for their services. This 'outside' status of accountants with their focus on financial accounting determined their training and professional mindset. Management accounting, the use of accounting to aid management decision making, to appraise processes and monitor performance against expectations, was not considered part of an accountant's training.[83] As with engineers the method of training was by pupillage. For accountants this was as an articled clerk though the Institute of Chartered Accountants of England and Wales (ICAEW) did have qualifying examinations from an early date. This ensured that a syllabus of study was covered but it largely excluded management accounting.

Generally, the attitude of business to accountants and accountancy was grudging. L. R. Dicksee, Professor of Accounting at the LSE wrote in 1915:

> . . . in general, a knowledge of accounts is not considered any part of the necessary education of a business officer, who accordingly is often quite ignorant of the uses that accountants have for him. On the contrary he is usually obsessed with the fixed idea that accounts are a necessary evil, that money spent on them is a sheer waste.[84]

But if their employers were grudging, the accountants employed by them were, according to Dicksee, quite content with a narrow role consistent with their training and the orientation of their profession:

> In too many cases the Accounts Department of a manufacturing business is entirely out of touch with practical requirements. Not infrequently it seems to glory in its isolation. In the majority of cases those connected with it seem to take a pride in dissociating themselves from the practical side of the business, and express a lofty contempt for it and its methods. Their ideal, and their sole ideal, is too often to build up annual accounts for submission to shareholders in general meeting . . .[85]

The picture presented, then, is of a specific niche for financial accountants within the firm created by external legislative and shareholder pressure. This is the view also of recent work on the history of accountants in UK industry.[86] It may be that the isolation of this niche was emphasised by the hostility to interference of manufacturing departments. Ultimately, however, the reason why financial accountants employed by manufacturing firms did not become involved in management accounting can only be that they were not required to do so by their employer. There appears to have been a prevalent view that the role of the financial accountant should be kept narrow. An English 'efficiency expert' wrote in 1919:

> An accountant should be kept in his place . . . accounting is a definite job which has to do with records only, and not with methods, loans, operations, policies or management . . . Accounting has on one side of it costing and on the other financing but there is a "twilight zone" between accounting and costing and also between accounting and finance and consequently the accountant sometimes gets out of his place and meddles with costing and finance, sometimes to the extent of monopolising all three jobs. This . . . is a very serious matter as the average accountant is quite unfit to handle costs or finance. Make your accountant stick to his Ledger; hire a special clerk for Costings and consult your banker on Finance.[87]

As this piece suggests UK firms kept costing – the basis or starting point of management accounting – organisationally separate from both the production and financial accounting departments. The origins of this separation appear to be the two main uses to which costing was put, namely estimating and the supervision of production. Given the commercial sensitivity of cost and price estimates it is not surprising that the principals of firms would wish to restrict access to the information. The use of costing, as an instrument of control of the directoral 'administrative' over the managerial 'executive' could not easily be delegated to the financial accountants without creating a *de facto* top management. The imposed division of labour, however, led to conflict and inefficiency:

> . . . with regard to the majority of cost accountants in this country . . . you will find that the cost accountant is debarred on the one side from knowledge of the financial accounts and on the other side from a proper knowledge of works processes and works organisations. The result is, you will find, the works and cost accountant has put up a certain set of figures, and he is slammed on one side by the works and on the other by the Board of Directors, so that between the two the majority of cost accountants do not know whether they are standing on their heads or their heels.[88]

Indeed, one cost accountant suggested in 1923 that the system was deliberately adversarial: 'The old manager's axiom was "Divide and Rule". It was a very safe game to play in those days to always pit one department against another.'[89] There is clear evidence, then, that the engineering and accounting professionals employed by UK manufacturers were organised in a way that kept them separate, with jobs that were narrow in scope and at times adversarial. There is a strong resemblance between the narrow scope and compartmentalised role of professionals and the water-tight departments of the railways that we considered above. The common factor is the proprietorial desire to reserve to the board the co-ordinating and other top management functions rather than delegate them to managers.

Consequences: rigidity and adaptability

The structures of large firms in our period were a clear consequence of a theoretical model of how firms should be managed. Particularly important results flowed from the prescribed split between the roles of managers and directors. Because control of the enterprise as a whole was reserved to the Board there was next to no development of top management, functional departments were rigidly separated and the scope of the technical professional's work was narrow. This limited the ability of organisations to produce innovative management structures and techniques and indeed to produce managers. The part-time role of the directors limited their scope to manage creatively and set limits to the scale or complexity of enterprises that could be managed under this form of organisation. As a worst case, the almost unassailable power of the directors combined with lack of delegation and bad or desultory decision-making on their part produced an almost irreversible decline of the firm.

The various structures actually adopted by large UK enterprise before World War One were the product of a tension between the proprietorial requirement that the firm be controlled by the directors and a commercial necessity to delegate to managers. This explains why, in banking for example, when the perceived commercial necessity of delegations diminished, power would be resumed by the board. It means that delegations to managers at this time were not the start of a Chandlerian progress towards the managerialist enterprise. Left undisturbed by further diversification or amalgamation the structure of some of the firms we have surveyed remained remarkably unchanged for many years. There were a considerable number of large companies which were essentially the same post World War Two as they were pre World War One, notably J and P Coats, English Sewing Cotton, Calico Printers Association, GKN, Imperial Tobacco and brewing companies generally. Even after very large amalgamations in the inter-war years, the railway companies retained most of the structural features of the pre-World War One companies.[90] We may conclude, therefore, that the proprietorial form of governance was not a transitional, short-lived form as long as the complexity or scale of the management task was within the capacity of the structure to cope with it. We can also see how rigid and resistant to change the structures of UK joint stock companies were essentially designed to be.

In itself this may merely be an interesting observation. The purpose of a business is to survive and prosper rather than to indulge in organisational experiments. Some at least of the firms in this list were in industrial sectors and types of markets which did not require particularly complex and fast changing management to survive. Nevertheless these firms were symptomatic of a wider ideology that firstly resisted change and when change came attempted to set narrow limits within which that change could take place. An examination of large firms in the inter-war years[91] shows how even in the midst of organic growth, amalgamation or organisational change certain assumptions on the prerogatives of proprietorial non-executive directors worked to weaken the effectiveness of the resulting structure. This applies to even the most 'advanced' firms like ICI, Unilever or the LMS Railway.

The question that faced evolving very large or complex firms was: how could they be controlled without losing competitive advantage either through bureaucratic rigidity or costly overheads? The response of large US or German corporations from the end of the nineteenth century onwards was to evolve the multi-divisional company. Typically these companies have decentralised divisions which contain all the functions necessary for an autonomous business – for example, accountancy, manufacturing and marketing – each function having divisional managers led by a divisional chief officer. The divisions are managed from a headquarters that has both line and functional control over them. The firm is headed by a chief executive and functional executive directors who all sit on the board and dominate it. Though the structure was expensive efficiencies were achieved through the deployment of new management techniques which the more intensively managed structures were able to develop. These efficiencies more than paid for the extra expense. Managed efficiently these structures could then grow without losing control and as yet no obvious upper limit to growth is apparent. The multi-divisional company is now the dominant organisational form of the companies making up the global oligopolies.[92] The corollary of this is that developed national economies that have historically failed to produce multi-divisional companies are potentially less competitive.

Set out in this schematic way it is clear that there are considerable differences between the organisational principles of the multi-divisional firm and the UK proprietorial firm. Firstly the distinction is ended between proprietor/directors on the one hand and employee/managers on the other. Secondly there is an integration of general management across the top of divisions and across the top of the firm as a whole. Thirdly the firm is both decentralised and controlled as opposed to the proprietorial alternatives of centralised control or federalism. Fourthly the main line of control is not through nomination of local boards of directors or some other relationship of ownership but through line management from the chief executive through the divisional chief officers and down through the organisation. Fifthly functional management is controlled throughout the organisation by head office setting out the procedures to be followed with line management responsible for enforcing compliance in the divisions. All these changes moved the power within the organisation away from proprietors to managers.[93]

Moving from the proprietorial to the managerial form proved extraordinarily difficult for large UK companies in the inter-war years. Boards generally continued to be appointed on a proprietorial rather than a functional basis. Chief executives as such rarely joined the Board and where they did so it was usually because they combined the role with another position – for example Josiah Stamp was both President of the Executive and Chairman of the Board on the LMS. Chief functional officers never joined the boards of firms in the inter-war years.[94] Some directors might take a particular interest in specific functions but despite a brief interlude at ICI when directors were made responsible for functional activities[95] and despite some advocates for the practice[96] functional directors did not become established from the board down (as opposed from the managers upwards) in this period either.

It has not proved possible to find examples of complete integration at management level of functions across the top of divisions in the inter-war years. ICI's divisions were decentralised but were for manufacturing only – marketing and finance being controlled elsewhere. Unilever's (centralised) divisions combined manufacturing and marketing but finance was a separate HQ department reporting to the executive committee of the board. Beyond these examples it is difficult to find UK firms with divisions, properly defined, in the inter-war years. As far as the top of the firm was concerned integration of management was never unambiguously established. At the LMS for example full time executive Vice Presidents ran groups of functional departments and met frequently under the leadership of the chief executive but the chief executive, as we have seen, was also the chairman. Furthermore the traditional railway board committees remained in place and cut across the jurisdiction of the Vice Presidents directly to the heads of departments. The result was an illogical melange of managerial and proprietorial firm structures. At ICI managerial integration at HQ level was minimal. While overall integral control of the company was formally the responsibility of the board, real control lay with the Chairman and Managing Director Harry McGowan working through small board committees dominated by him. At Unilever all matters of substance were decided by an executive committee of the board representing a balance of proprietorial interests sitting in almost permanent session which was attended by senior managers from product divisions in rotation.

There was really only one company with decentralised divisions – albeit restricted to manufacturing – and that was ICI. Control of these divisions from HQ was problematic. McGowan's word could reach any part of the organisation but the firm was simply too vast for one-man management. Once established the divisions proved intractable in terms of technical development and financial control and their ability to adapt to changing commercial circumstances. On the other hand the divisions could with justification have pleaded that they received little from HQ in terms of information or support. Planning and reporting mechanisms were weak and so, more significantly, were line and functional management. ICI was paradoxically personally over-centralised and managerially under-controlled.

The issue of line management – in its simplest terms the rights of some to give orders to others – was not a pressing matter in proprietorial companies. This was the case even when they reached a considerable size – see the railways for example – and in many cases it did not matter whether companies were centralised or federal because it was clear where authority lay. Functional management on the other hand was an emerging problem after World War One even when firms were centralised. If all authority was reserved to the board or its committees and radiated from them to departmental managers a technical department at HQ could not instruct some section – a factory or a sales team – on how they should proceed. Instructions had to come from directors who were increasingly limited in the time they could give to detail as firms became larger and more complex. This left HQ technical departments in an awkward position. At ICI and Unilever which unlike many companies were explicit on the matter the status of technical departments was 'advisory' and they and the divisions were supposed to make arrangements work by mutual consent. Even finance departments which had considerable directorial backing could not compel adherence in their own right. The amorphous nature of technical authority became more sharply apparent when attempts were made to decentralise, particularly when there was little line management structure in which to place technical functions.

This discussion illustrates the difficulties faced when proprietorial ideology attempted to deal with technical complexity combined with large scale and scope of business activity. Increased scope pointed to divisionalisation as a rational response. Scale implied delegation/ decentralisation of tasks. Technical complexity demanded consistent procedures across the technical departments of the enterprise. If this was to be achieved without departmental balkanisation technical departments had to be placed within a unified line management structure while central technical departments set out common procedures which line management enforced. The proprietorial mindset could accept some parts of this organisational package but not the whole of it. The most aware commentators in the inter-war years knew that UK big business faced great problems in dealing with scale, scope and increasing functional complexity[97] yet both they and the most 'progressive' large UK businesses with the managerialist examples of the US before them[98] would not indeed *could not* consider them as models. The reason is ultimately very simple: the managerialist structure threatened the power of the proprietorial director and thus was not acceptable. The choice of managerial or proprietorial model was not, of course, offered in such an obvious way. Indeed, as far as one is able to judge the 'managerialist model' was not understood as such until World War Two and beyond.[99] Firms adopted the organisational ideas of others pragmatically or innovated under pressure according to the possible courses of action they felt were open to them. The significance of the proprietorial theory of the firm was that it conditioned which options a UK firm could consider possible. Combined with a partially and then fully protected and cartellised economy in the 1920s and 1930s followed by the closed economy of World War and the sellers market thereafter[100] the proprietorial theory of the firm was a further disincentive to adaptation and change. It is not surprising that the accommodations of proprietorial directors to the imperatives of growth and complexity were grudging and minimal. Proprietorial directorial power and the theory it produced and from which it drew support thus did more than simply result in a less than optimal organisational response at the level of the firm to changing business conditions. It was an important contributory factor to a maladaptive business culture that left the UK sliding into crisis and relative decline when the evolving competitive global economy began to burst over UK business from the late 1950s onwards.

Appendix: large companies in 1905

A number of authors have developed lists of large companies for different points in the Twentieth Century. Sources are set out at note 32. The tendency has been to exclude services and consider manufacturing separately. The notable exception is Peter Wardly. The extant lists are for service and manufacturing companies together ordered by market value, manufacturing companies by capitalisation, and manufacturing companies by numbers employed. In order to give a representative sample of large enterprise prior to World War One it has been found prudent to consider a further list of service and manufacturing companies ordered by capitalisation. This is set out below.

Largest 50 UK Companies by Capitalisation, c. 1905

Company	Capitalisation (£000's)
1. Midland Railway Co	191,051
2. London and Northwestern Railway Co	122,825
3. Great Western Railway Co	92,806
4. North Eastern Railway Co	78,006
5. Lancashire and Yorkshire Railway Co	68,001

Largest 50 UK Companies by Capitalisation, c. 1905

Company	Capitalisation (£000's)
6. Caledonian Railway Co	66,660
7. North British Railway Co	63,939
8. Great Northern Railway Co	58,385
9. Great Eastern Railway Co	54,207
10. London and Southwestern Railway Co	50,421
11. Great Central Railway Co	46,678
12. South Eastern Railway Co	32,075
13. London Chatham & Dover Railway Co	28,629
14. London Brighton & South Coast Railway Co	27,991
15. Gas Light & Coke Co	25,797
16. Glasgow & South Western Railway Co	24,630
17. London and India Docks	18,975
18. Imperial Tobacco	17,545
19. Manchester Ship Canal	16,603
20. Metropolitan Railway Co	15,764
21. Watney Combe Reid	14,950
22. Bank of England	14,553
23. Great Southern & Western Railway Co (Ireland)	13,381
24. Metropolitan District Railway Co	12,407
25. J & P Coats	11,181
26. National Telephone Co	10,833
27. North Staffordshire Railway Co	10,454
28. Underground Electric Railway Co	10,200
29. Taff Vale Railway Co	9,421
30. South Metropolitan Gas Co	8,820
31. United Alkali	8,490
32. Great Northern of Ireland Railway Co	8,267
33. Calico Printers Association	8,227
34. Eastern Telegraph Co	7,897
35. Furness Railway Co	7,818
36. Hull & Barnsley Railway Co	7,669
37. Great North of Scotland Railway Co	7,611
38. Vickers Sons & Maxim	7,440
39. Fine Cotton Spinners and Doublers	7,290
40. Associated Portland Cement Manufacturers	7,061
41. Highland Railway Co	6,824
42. Bleachers Association	6,820
43. Midland Great Western of Ireland Railway Co	6,511
44. Cambrian Railway	6,306
45. Arthur Guinness	5,960
46. Barry Railway	5,790
48. Sir W G Armstrong Whitworth	5,316
49. Samuel Allsopp & Sons	5,095
50. Imperial Continental Gas Co	4,964

Source: P L Payne "Emergence of the Large-Scale Company in Great Britain, 1870–1914" in Economic History Review 2nd Series, XX, 3 December 1967 with the addition of companies taken from Peter Wardley's lists of market values (q.v.) with capitalisations from the Stock Exchange Year Book for 1905.

A sample has been derived by taking the above list with the list by market value and by employment. There is no particularly scientific method for selecting groups of companies from the three lists. The railways clearly form a dominant group. The banks form a strong group in the list by market value. Of the remaining companies after these two groups in the lists by capitalisation and by market value the next strongest group is amalgamated manufacturing companies. If the top 20, say, manufacturing employers are examined for amalgamated manufacturing companies, we can identify ten, the balance being railway or railway related, state enterprise, the CWS or family companies. Taking the amalgamated manufacturing companies from the three lists a certain pattern emerges:

By Capitalisation	By Market Value	By Numbers Employed
Imperial Tobacco	J & P Coats	Fine Cotton Spinners
Watney Combe Reid	Imperial Tobacco	Armstrong Whitworth
J & P Coats	Vickers	Vickers
United Alkali	Armstrong Whitworth	Calico Printers Assoc
Calico Printers Assoc	Watney Combe Reid	John Brown & Co
Vickers	Fine Cotton Spinners	J & P Coats
Fince Cotton Spinners		GKN
Associated Portland Cement		Bleachers Association
Bleachers Association		United Alkali
Armstrong Whitworth		Stewarts & Lloyds

We can establish four broad groups in the steel, shipbuilding and armaments conglomerations (Vickers, Armstrong Whitworth, John Brown); brewing and tobacco (Imperial Tobacco, Watney Combe Reid); textiles and textile finishing (J & P Coats, Calico Printers Assoc., Fine Cotton spinners and Doublers, Bleachers Assoc.) and a miscellaneous group (Associated Portland Cement Manufacturers, United Alkali, Guest Keen & Nettlefold, Stewart and Lloyds).

It is not proposed to deal with the brewing and tobacco group since they were simple and straightforwardly proprietorial. As far as Imperial Tobacco is concerned, for example, a loose holding company was ideal and integration was clearly the last thing on the participants' minds. (See the remarks of Sir Wilfred Anson, deputy Chair of Imperial Tobacco in *Business Enterprise*, R. S. Edwards and W. Townsend, London, pp. 65–6.) The brewery industry's position in the lists was largely the consequence of the artificially high values placed on retail outlets – the public houses – as a result of restrictions on licenses by magistrates.

Their organisations were simply unitary board structures made up of the partners of the amalgamating companies. (See J. Vaizey *The Brewery Industry 1886–1951*, London.)

It is also not proposed to deal with the miscellaneous gas companies, insurance companies, extraction companies and others that form the balance of the capitalisation and market value lists. The groups extracted above appear to provide a sufficient basis for what is intended to be an illustrative survey.

Notes

* This paper presents a summary of one theme of my doctoral thesis: J. M. Quail, 'Proprietors and Managers: Structure and Technique in large British enterprise 1890 to 1930' (unpublished Ph.D. thesis, University of Leeds, 1996).

1 The use of the word 'ideology' is designed to set a different context from that of, say, 'culture'. Culture may be defined as a set of implicit ideas which explain social action but too often the culture is inferred from the social action itself. This is dangerously close to tautology. Ideology is here understood to be a more explicit set of ideas impelling social action: 'ideas at the basis of some economic or political theory or system.' (Oxford Concise Dictionary).

2 See the survey by N. R. Lamoreaux, D. M. G. Raff and P. Temin, 'New Economic Approaches to the Study of Business History' *Business and Economic History*, 26, 1, 1997.

3 See for example D. C. Coleman 'The Uses and Abuses of Business History', *Business History*, XXIX, 1987. Note however some more recent work of a more theoretical bent discussed in J. F. Wilson, *British Business History, 1720–1994* (Manchester: Manchester University Press, 1995), Chapter 1.

4 See the arguments of the 'institutionalist' contributors to B. Elbaum and W. Lazonick (eds) *The Decline of the British Economy* (Oxford: Clarendon Press, 1986). The sectors with which the contributors deal for the most part are the old competitive staples cotton and steel. A large bank or railway or oligopolistic manufacturing company, however, had ceased to have to conform to those before and after it in the market co-ordinated supply and demand chain.

5 'Proprietors' was the name used by pre-World War One railways to describe their shareholders, and the 'Court of Proprietors' was the name given by the Bank of England and some older insurance companies to their board of directors. The use of the word is designed to emphasise the property rights which legitimised the director's role. My use of the word 'proprietorial' should not be confused with W. Lazonick's term 'proprietary'. See W. Lazonick, *Business Organisation and the Myth of the Market Economy* (Cambridge: Cambridge University Press, 1991), pp. 23–7. Lazonick is concerned to distinguish between owner-managed (or proprietary) capitalism and managerial capitalism. My suggestion is that there was an intermediate – and long-lasting – stage between these types of capitalism in the UK.

6   H. Goitein, *Company Law* (London: Pitman, 1949), p. 142. See generally pp. 131–169 for subsequent paragraphs unless otherwise stated. Cases used as illustrations are all pre-1929. Direct quotes are referenced.

7   Goitein, *Company Law*, p. 160.

8   Goitein, *Company Law*, p. 158.

9   See J. B. Jefferys, 'Business Organisation in Great Britain 1856–1914' (unpublished Ph.D. thesis, University of London, 1938), reprinted Arno Press, New York 1977. But cf. P. L. Cottrell, *Industrial Finance 1830–1914* (London: Methuen, 1980), particularly Chapter 4. Cottrell suggests that the extensive use of preferred shares with limited voting rights pre-empted the scope of shareholder control. The difference between the authors is one of degree: the simple fact that there was a large market for preferred shares with more guaranteed returns but limited power also suggests that investors were increasingly indifferent to active involvement.

10   D. Crane, *Sir Robert Perks, Bart, MP – The Story of his Life* (London: Culley, 1909), p. 63. Perks had been involved in companies, he said, with aggregate capital of more than £150 million.

11   Scott Lings, *Trade Combination*, quoted in J. F. Wilson, *Ferranti and the British Electrical Industry, 1864–1930* (Manchester: Manchester University Press, 1988), p. 63.

12   Jefferys, 'business organisation', pp. 402–3.

13   Quotation from *Railway News*, 18 February 1905, in G. Alderman, *The Railway Interest* (Leicester: University Press, 1973), p. 227. See also discussion pp. 26–8.

14   *Economist*, 20 July 1912, p. 110.

15   *Accountant*, 13 September 1930, article 'Director's Qualifications'.

16   Quoted in W. J. Reader, *ICI: A History* (Oxford: Oxford University Press, 1970), Vol. 1, pp. 270–1.

17   Goitein, p. 161.

18   Table A, the model articles of association in the companies acts, forbade the taking of such positions by directors up to 1908 when the position of managing director was allowed.

19   Herbert W. Jordan, *ABC Guide to the Companies Acts 1862 to 1907* (London: Jordan, 1908), p. 31.

20   Edward Williams, ex-manager of Bolckow Vaughan, speaking in 1879, quoted in D. L. Burn, *The Economic History of Steel Making 1867–1939* (Cambridge: Cambridge University Press, 1940), p. 256.

21   Goitein, *Company Law*, pp. 159–160.

22   See for example the case *In re National Bank of Wales Ltd*, Goitein, pp. 161–2.

23   See the important Marzetti case of 1880 where a director of a firm in liquidation was held liable to repay money wrongly paid out on the basis of deceitful assurances by other directors. It was held that he should have known from the circumstances that the payment was wrongful. See Goitein, *Company Law*, p. 165.

24   *Economist*, 27 May 1911, Letter from Mr Reg. Murray.

25   *Economist*, 20 July 1912, p. 10.

26   L. Urwick, *The Meaning of Rationalisation* (London: Nisbet, 1929), pp. 115–16. The quote is from O. Sheldon, *The Philosophy of Management* (London: Pitman, 1924), p. 32.

27 *Economist*, 27 May 1911 (letter from Mr Reg. Murray) and 3 June 1911 (letter from Mr Herbert Hill) warns of the dangers of take-overs by managing directors or general managers given powers which properly belong to the board.
28 L. R. Dicksee, *Business Organisation* (London: Longmans, 1910), p. 49.
29 John Lee 'Industrial Structure VII. The Value of Comparisons', *Business Organisation and Management*, 6, 4 July 1922.
30 L. Urwick, *Rationalisation*, pp. 137–8. It is presumed that the 'weekly board meeting' referred to is some kind of management committee.
31 A list of companies for both services and manufacturing ranked by market value is given by Peter Wardley, 'The Anatomy of Big Business: Aspects of Corporate Development in the Twentieth Century', *Business History*, 33, 2 April 1991. A list of manufacturing companies ranked by capitalisation is given in P. L. Payne, 'Emergence of the Large-scale Company in Great Britain, 1870–1914', *Economic History Review*, 2nd series, XX, 3, 1967. A list of manufacturing companies ranked by numbers employed is given by Christine Shaw, 'The Large Manufacturing Employers of 1907', *Business History*, 25, 1, 1983. A list of manufacturing and service companies compiled by the author is given at the section Appendix: large companies in 1905.
32 See Barry Supple, *Royal Exchange Assurance* (Cambridge: Cambridge University Press, 1970), pp. 68–70, 349–50. See also the Seventeenth and Eighteenth Century trading companies described in Ann M. Carlos and Stephen Nicholas 'Giants of an Earlier Capitalism, The Chartered Trading Companies as Modern Multinationals', *Business History Review*, 62, 3, Autumn 1988.
33 M. R. Bonavia, *The Economics of Transport* (London: Nisbet, 1936), p. 74.
34 Ray Morris, *Railroad Administration* (London: Appleton, 1910), p. 125.
35 W. R. Lawson, *British Railways, A Financial and Commercial Survey* (London: Constable, 1913), p. 238.
36 PRO RAIL 527 Index.
37 PRO RAIL 491 Index and Director's Diaries PRO RAIL 491/1139/17 and PRO RAIL 491/1139/18. Samples from Board Minutes 1899–1905 (PRO RAIL 491/28) and 1917–1923 (PRO RAIL 491/31).
38 1907 taken as sample year. See e.g. Board Minutes 15 February 1907, PRO RAIL 410/40. If anything, the numbers of outside bodies had dropped.
39 Taken from PRO RAIL 410/1268.
40 There is a representative example at PRO RAIL 410/345 LNWR General Finance Committee 1904–1909.
41 See for example Lord Claud Hamilton, Chairman of the Great Eastern Railway in *The Times*, 14 February 1914, p. 20: '. . . all our railway systems were divided in what he would call water-tight departments. The traffic, goods, engineering and other departments were kept so apart that as a rule there was very little interchange from one to another on the part of the young men employed. The inevitable effect of that was to remove on the part of these young men any incentive to new ideas and new methods.' It does not seem to have occurred to the noble lord that as chairman he might do something about the situation.
42 This is the phrase used by Joseph Sykes, *The Amalgamation Movement in British Banking 1825–1924* (London: King, 1926).

43 A. R. Holmes and Edwin Green, *Midland – 150 Years of Banking Business* (London: Batsford, 1986), Chapter 4.

44 P. W. Mathews and A. W. Tuke, *History of Barclays Bank Ltd* (London: Blades, 1926).

45 R. S. Sayers, *Lloyds Bank in the History of English Banking* (Oxford: Clarendon Press, 1957); J. R. Winton, *Lloyds Bank 1918–1969* (Oxford: Oxford University Press, 1982).

46 Holmes and Green, *Midland*, p. 112 ff.

47 J. F. Davis, *Bank Organisation Management and Accounts* (London: Pitman, 1910), p. 65.

48 Homes and Green, *Midland Bank*, Chapter 4.

49 See P. L. Cottrell, *Industrial Finance*, p. 168, for breweries. For Imperial Tobacco see B. W. E. Alford, *W. D. and H. O. Wills and the Development of the UK Tobacco Industry* (London: Methuen, 1977).

50 See Macrosty *Trust Movement*, pp. 40–45 for the detailed history of acquisitions. See also Clive Trebilcock, *Vickers Brothers – Armaments and Enterprise 1854–1914* (London: Europa, 1977) and J. R. Hume and M. S. Moss, *Beardmore – The History of a Scottish Industrial Giant* (London: Heinemann, 1979).

51 See L. Hannah, 'Strategy and Structure in the Manufacturing Sector' in L. Hannah (ed.), *Management Strategy and Business Development* (London: Methuen, 1976).

52 See figures in Macrosty *Trust Movement*, pp. 41 and 43. For the remainder of this paragraph see the discussion in Quail, 'proprietors and managers', pp. 57–59.

53 Introduction to Vickers Papers Index, Tyne and Wear Archives, Newcastle upon Tyne.

54 In 1908 there were nine Coats family directors and three from the acquired firms. In addition there were two outside directors from Coats' flotation in 1890 and the Sales Director of Coats, O. E. Philippi and his son. By 1914 one Coats family member and one outside director had been lost and the balance had not changed. (Source: *Stock Exchange Year Book*).

55 A. Slaven, S. Checkland (eds), *Dictionary of Scottish Business Biography 1860–1980*, Vol. 1, entries for Otto Ernst Philippi and Archibald Coats. For the international ramifications of Coats see Dong-Woon Kim, 'J and P Coats as a Multinational before 1914', *Business and Economic History*, 26, 2, 1997.

56 See Macrosty *Trust Movement*, Chapter 5.

57 Macrosty *Trust Movement*, p. 140. However, the FCSD appears to have become more centralised under a powerful Managing Director by 1909. See J. F. Wilson, *British Business History, 1720–1994* (Manchester: Manchester University Press, 1995), p. 107. It is not clear whether this was a return to the comforts of the past through a kind of neo-proprietor or a version of the J & P Coats situation where an exceptional individual was given personal powers but always subject to the approval of a powerful board.

58 Macrosty *Trust Movement*. p. 141.

59 Macrosty *Trust Movement*. p. 143.

60 The Bleachers Association, J. & P. Coats and Horrockses Crewdson and Co. were represented on the CPA investigation committee that said in its report

that the representatives of three successful amalgamations viewed a statistical department as essential. The committee also recommended centralisation of buying and finance and central control of expenditure. See footnote 62.

61 The CPA investigation committee report is given in full in Macrosty *Trust Movement*, Appendix IV. References from this for subsequent treatment of CPA.

62 Macrosty *Trust Movement*, pp. 108–116 and P. L. Cook and R. Cohen, *Effects of Mergers* (London: Allen and Unwin, 1958), Section I.

63 Edgar Jones, *GKN* (Basingstoke: Macmillan, 1987), Vol. I, p. 365.

64 A. D. Chandler, *Scale and Scope* (Cambridge MA, Belknap Harvard, 1990), passim.

65 This is the view of L. Urwick and E. F. L. Brech, *The Making of Scientific Management: Vol. II Management in British Industry* (London: Management Publications Trust, 1946).

66 W. H. G. Armytage, *Social History of Engineering* (London: Faber, 1969), pp. 235–6.

67 R. H. Parsons, *History of the Institution of Mechanical Engineers* (London: Institution of Mechanical Engineers, 1947), p. 34 – the grounds for opposition appear to stem from the idea that it was a practical, not a theoretical, profession.

68 See the comments of Sir Frank Gill and Prof. Goodman in Chapter VIII of Urwick and Brech, *Scientific Management* and the exam papers detailed in Parsons, *Mechanical Engineers*, p. 47.

69 W. A. J. O'Meara, 'The Future of the Engineer – His Education and Training' in E. T. Elbourne, *The Costing Problem* (London: Library Press, 1919), p. 123.

70 This picture emerges vividly from the pages of J. E. Powell, *The Output Problem* (London: Library Press, 1920). See also letter from D. W. Myers in *Engineering Production*, I, 4, April 4, 1920, p. 165 on progress clerks.

71 See the entry for Engineers in Duncan Cross, *Choosing a Career* (London: Cassell, 1908), p. 158 ff.

72 Sir Lynden Macassey quoted in O. Sheldon, *Philosophy of Management*, p. 71.

73 See e.g. the interesting discussion in Manchester of a reading of W. A. J. O'Meara's paper (as footnote 70) to local electrical engineers in *Journal of the Institution of Electrical Engineers* (JIEE), 57, 280, March 1919.

74 As footnote 73: contribution of P. M. Baker.

75 Anne Loft, *Coming Into the Light* (London: Chartered Institute of Management Accountants, 1990), p. 8.

76 *Engineer*, quoted Urwick and Brech, *Scientific Management Vol. II*, p. 118.

77 *Second Report on Costs and Efficiencies for H M Factories* (London: Ministry of Munitions, 1918).

78 J. Slater Lewis, *The Commercial Organisation of Factories* (London: Spon, 1896), has an organisation chart showing costing staff reporting to the general manager rather than the works manager. E. T. Elbourne, *Factory Administration and Accounts* (London: Longmans, 1914) has the works accountant responsible to the financial manager who in turn is responsible to the board rather than the general manager.

79 Sir Herbert Austin, 'The General Value of Cost Control', *Accountant*, 19 June 1920, p. 721. He was later to dismiss the idea that he had ever said such a thing. See *Cost Accountant*, 4, 12 May 1925, p. 420.

80 Yorkshire Local Section Chair, W. Long, JIEE, 56, 269, December 1917.

81 A. S. E. Ackerman, J I E E, 57, 280, March 1919. (Discussion of O'Meara's paper as footnote 73).

82 See Chapter 2 of Edgar Jones, *Accountancy and the British Economy 1840–1980* (London: Batsford, 1981), for the next paragraph. See also footnote 86.

83 See L. R. Dicksee's analysis of the examination papers for the ICAEW in his *Fundamentals of Manufacturing Costs* (London: Gee, 1917), pp. 5, 6.

84 L. R. Dicksee, *Business Methods and the War* (Cambridge: Cambridge University Press, 1915), p. 19.

85 L. R. Dicksee, *Fundamentals*, p. 5.

86 D. Matthews, M. Anderson, J. R. Edwards, *The Priesthood of Industry – the Rise of the Professional Accountant in British Management*,(Oxford: Oxford University Press, 1998). This identifies the key factors in the rise of professional accounting in the Victorian and Edwardian years as the rise of the limited liability company and the need for checks by 'management' (directors?) on employees 'and by shareholders on both these groups' (p. 139). The niche that accountants established in UK companies was later to prove an important bridgehead for the profession in UK management after World War Two.

87 H. Casson writing in *Efficiency*, quoted in *Accountant*, March 1, 1919, p. 1.

88 Morley Mower, *Cost Accountant*, 1, 10, March 1922, p. 191.

89 Robert Stelling, 'What Good Management Involves', *Cost Accountant*, 3, 5 October 1923.

90 See Quail, 'proprietors and managers', Chapter 5. For other than railway companies see Graham Turner, *Business in Britain* (London: Eyre and Spottiswoode, 1969); R. S. Edwards and H. Townsend, Business Enterprise (London: Macmillan, 1958); *idem, Studies in Business Organisation* (London: Macmillan, 1961).

91 Quail, 'proprietors and managers', Part 2.

92 It is significant that while earlier Japanese corporations based on the old trading companies have retained strong elements of a distinct Japanese company structure (W. M. Fruin, *The Japanese Enterprise System* (Oxford: Oxford University Press, 1992)) more recent companies like Sony have moved directly to the multi-divisional type (see Y. Suzuki, *Japanese Management Structures 1920–80* (London: Macmillan, 1991).) I have argued elsewhere (Quail, 'proprietors and managers', Introduction) that globalisation has tended to iron out national corporate differences so that they simply become relatively minor variations of multi-divisional structures.

93 A. D. Chandler, *The Visible Hand* (Cambridge MA: Belknap Harvard, 1977); A. D. Chandler, *Scale and Scope* (Cambridge MA: Belknap Harvard, 1990).

94 The pioneers of this development, finance directors, did not emerge until the 1950s and 1960s: Matthews, Anderson and Edwards, *Priesthood*, p. 215.

95 Quail, 'proprietors and managers', for this and following passages unless otherwise referenced.

96 For example John Lee, *Letters to an Absentee Director* (London: Pitman, 1928).

97 L. Urwick 'Executive Decentralisation with Functional Co-ordination', *Public Administration*, 13 October 1935.

98 There was considerable traffic between US and UK large corporations. ICI was close to DuPont and their archives contain reports on developments in DuPont's structure. Executives at LMS took regular trips to the USA to look at developments on US railroads. Austin toured US car plants. Unilever had a US subsidiary from which lessons – though mainly on product ranges and marketing – were drawn.

99 Changes at the political level were analysed by James Burnham, *The Managerial Revolution* (New York: 1941). The divergence of ownership and control in large US corporations was analysed by A. A. Berle and G. C. Means, *The Modern Corporation and Private Property* (New York: Macmillan, 1932). But this is only the start of the matter. Discussions in management literature appear to have concentrated on issues of centralisation or decentralisation. It could be argued that it was not until the publication of *The Visible Hand* that the structures of companies were discussed in terms of the social groups they favoured.

100 Helen Mercer, *Constructing a Competitive Order* (Cambridge: Cambridge University Press, 1995), particularly chapter 2.

Afterword

John Quail

This piece was an attempt to set out how one particular theory of the firm, to all appearances rational, consistent and coherent, could arrive at such dysfunctional outcomes. It ends with the view that having been preserved through Depression and World War Two this 'maladaptive business culture' was sliding into crisis in the newly exposed international competitive conditions of the 1950s. Further work, as yet unpublished, since 'the proprietorial theory' appeared, demonstrates that this crisis was real enough and declarations in the literature of renaissance and recovery in the 1980s and 1990s were hopeful rather than sustainable: UK companies continued to manifest dysfunctial organisational structures, insufficiently skilled and co-ordinated human capital and rigidity and lack of adaptability in the face not only of competition but a competition that had manifestly found better ways to proceed and had done so for years.

Chapter 4

Trust in an industrial district

The Potteries, c. 1850–1900

Andrew Popp

The concept of the industrial district has enjoyed a long renaissance since its revival at the hands of Piore, Sabel and Zeitlin in the mid-1980s,[1] figuring prominently in the work of business and social historians,[2] economic geographers,[3] regional development scholars and others.[4] Much of this literature presents a highly positive picture of the industrial district. Industrial districts are said to foster business networks which hold out a range of 'strategic promises' to participants and drive growth throughout the regional economy.[5] In particular, it is argued, industrial districts generate high levels of trust, leading to the emergence of a creative and distinctive balance of co-operation and competition. However, this school of thought has not been without its critics. Taplin and Winterton, for example, have accused Piore, Sabel and Zeitlin of 'euphoria', of producing little more than '"fables"' that make 'enchanting reading'.[6] More recently, Joseph Melling has commented that Sabel and Zeitlin's work continues to lack a 'compelling version of how political and economic regimes are constituted', and that the effectiveness of the response made by craft-oriented firms and industries to the rise of mass production in the late nineteenth century remains 'open to serious debate'.[7]

Some of the shortcomings of the model are acknowledged by its proponents. Staber, whilst arguing that the business networks of industrial districts are characterised by a distinctive degree of 'social embeddedness', goes on to note that:

> Without an explanation of the process by which actors come to see themselves as network participants the district concept of social embeddedness remains theoretically empty. In short, the idea of social embeddedness leads to important questions about how actors build an account of the network that forms the basis for behaving co-operatively and innovatively.[8]

As a result, the concept is 'silent on the content of social relations (and) on the *mechanisms* by which social structures constrain or facilitate economic action'.[9] As Melling's observation suggests, the precise ways in which district networks are constituted, especially their social and cultural dimensions, remain hard to get at. This work contributes to these debates by focusing on the central concept of trust in the context of the North Staffordshire Potteries in the second half of the nineteenth century. Can the business culture of the Potteries industrial district be characterised, as the model would predict, as a high-trust culture? Did trust levels decline in this period and if so why? In order to explore these issues the four determinants of the level of trust within a culture postulated by Mark Casson will be deployed.[10] By isolating a range of factors this approach will allow the constitution of the Potteries industrial district to be delineated with more precision and any change observed in levels of trust addressed. Moreover, because, as Casson argues, 'Other things being equal, high levels of trust promote economic performance', exploration of these issues also permits reflection on the competitive performance of the British pottery industry at a crucial point in its history.[11]

The Potteries in the nineteenth century form an ideal site for an attempt to critically probe the conditions under which high levels of trust are likely to emerge. By the mid-nineteenth century the six townships of Stoke-on-Trent had developed a dense network of many largely small and medium-sized firms. Drawing on rich and highly localised pools of resources and capital, utilising flexible technologies, dependent on highly skilled workers and producing high-quality goods in batches, these firms dominated international markets for ceramic wares of every grade. Potting similarly dominated every aspect of life in the region, suffusing the working and domestic lives of the majority of the population and the social and political institutions of the district. In the last quarter of the century, however, the industry encountered an increasingly hostile environment. Foreign competition rose, tariff-barriers were erected in important export markets and prices experienced sustained downward pressure. Rates of business failure increased and heightened uncertainty became an established feature of potting life.

The response of the industry as a whole was weak. North Staffordshire's record in innovation, particularly process innovation, was unimpressive. Mechanisation was slow, hesitant and uneven. Developments in marketing strategies and in the internal organisation and governance of firms were equally tentative. Britain began to lose its international competitive advantage in ceramics, relinquishing control of important export markets and suffering the onset of import penetration. Most dramatic and damaging was the fall in the value of exports to its most valuable overseas market, the US. Between 1890 and 1898 the value of exports to the US fell from around £900,000 p.a. to little more than £500,000 p.a. This fall cannot be attributed simply to the imposition of tariffs, for, as Stern makes clear, the share of their domestic market held by American pottery manufacturers fell just as sharply in this period. German firms were the beneficiaries, their prices sufficiently low to negate the impact of tariffs.[12] It was in this context that debate on the industry's problems rapidly uncovered growing levels of distrust within the district. Price competition between local firms intensified dramatically as businesses repeatedly undercut one another to gain scarce orders and gave hidden discounts for cash, copying of competitors designs at the suggestion of buyers became more common and buyer-supplier relations between firms within the district became increasingly opportunistic. At the same time, numerous attempted co-operative measures foundered on this newly exposed atmosphere of distrust. It is important to stress that it is not suggested that trust was low in any absolute sense, but only that it was falling, though to an extent that alarmed many.

The work is organised in six sections. In the first a historiographical survey will trace the emergence of trust as a central feature of the industrial district concept. Casson's postulated determinants of trust levels within a culture will then be introduced. The second section will begin with a detailed reconstruction of the business structure of the Potteries from about 1860 to 1890. It will be shown that the firm population of the industry was increasingly mobile and unstable. Examination of the business records of Jesse Shirley and Sons, a supplier of bone and other important inputs to ceramic production, will then enable these structural patterns to be related to change in the behaviour of firms. In the fourth section two issues will be explored. Firstly, the issue of time preferences will be addressed. Secondly, the extent to which the business culture of the Potteries was embedded in a wider culture of laissez-faire political economy, stressing the competitive discipline of impersonal free markets, will be considered. This will then be contrasted with the clear and growing tension between large and small firms within the industry. These tensions will form the focus of the fifth section, detailing the collapse of collaborative initiatives between the late 1850s and the early 1880s. The industry palpably failed to develop or demonstrate a sense of collective identity through these bodies. Tensions focused not only on the perceived negative economic impact of small firms, but also on issues of legitimacy and representativeness, allowing access to some of the meanings attached by potters to their participation in district networks.

Finally, a concluding section will reflect on the experience of the Potteries and on the position of trust within the industrial district concept.

I

All recent work on industrial districts, theoretical and empirical, has its roots in the pioneering work of Alfred Marshall. However, there are clear and important differences between the observations offered by Marshall and the 'model' formulated by modern proponents.[13] These differences are pointed up by Langlois and Robertson when they describe the 'Marshallian industrial district' as 'highly competitive in the neo-classical sense'.[14] This emphasis on very strong competitive forces *within* the district sits uneasily alongside the emphasis on co-operation found in the work of Piore *et al*. Indeed, the concept of trust finds no explicit place in Marshall's work. Marshall did recognise that the slow growth of industries in particular localities often led to the emergence of a strong 'industrial atmosphere, such as that of Sheffield or Solingen'.[15] The principal role played by this 'atmosphere' was in shaping human resource endowments, providing a pool of skilled and easily trained and supervised workers and an equal supply of potential entrepreneurs with an intimate knowledge of the trade. Thus, these atmospheres 'which cannot be quickly acquired, . . . yield gratis to the manufacturers . . . great advantages, that are not easily to be had elsewhere: and an atmosphere cannot be moved'.[16] Marshall clearly viewed the structure, resources and capabilities of each industrial district to be historically and spatially specific. Further, he recognised that patterns of personal relationship could reinforce these specificities, arguing that 'personal contact is most needed in trade between allied branches'.[17] This does not, however, amount to a carefully delineated concept of, or role for, trust within the industrial district.

Trust is, however, to the fore in the work of Piore, Sabel and Zeitlin. As Staber notes, their 'analysis of territorially bounded networking goes beyond standard agglomeration . . . reasoning by emphasising the *qualitative* social and institutional factors which facilitate quantitative external economies of co-location'.[18] In other words, their model privileges socio-cultural factors, giving them a more instrumental role than Marshall assigns to 'industrial atmosphere'. Trust is amongst the most important of these factors. They argue that in the industrial districts of the nineteenth century, 'each new generation (through) automatic and collective induction . . . learned the rules of competition and whom they could trust to abide by them (creating) a community across and within generations that protected the economy as a whole against the consequences of short-term calculations of advantage'.[19] That is to say, the way in which industrial districts were constituted in socio-cultural terms automatically promoted trust and foreclosed on forms of business behaviour that might have been damaging to the district as a whole.

Piore, Sabel and Zeitlin do not, however, specify in any great detail the mechanisms by which high levels of trust are generated, or sustained as conditions change. Moreover, empirical observation has cast doubt on the prevalence of trust within industrial districts. Enright, for example, claims that 'such trust is often both overstated and overrated . . . I have yet to see a case in which trust has caused behaviour that was inconsistent with the parties self-interest'.[20] Reality rarely seems able to support Harrison's simple linear model that runs from 'proximity to experience to trust to collaboration to enhanced regional economic growth'.[21] Staber, building on the work of Granovetter, has sought to address these shortcomings through use of the concept of social embeddedness. His argument runs thus:

> from a social embeddedness perspective, co-location implies an additional quality (to standard agglomeration theory), of a sort that gives firms the incentive to interact in a trustworthy manner . . . In summary, the industrial district model views social embeddedness as the key to what would normally be considered a contradictory combination of competition and cooperation.[22]

What, then, are the conditions under which a high level of trust between economic actors is likely to emerge and what relationship, if any, do these conditions have to spatial clustering? Mark Casson has developed a series of specific postulates that may help us to address these questions. Interestingly, these suggest that proximity, or at least familiarity, is an important determinant of the level of trust within a society.[23] Thus, his first postulate, that 'Immobility . . . promotes an atmosphere of trust', precedes from the argument that in an 'immobile society individuals expect to encounter one another repeatedly, and so find it economic to invest in a reputation for good behaviour'.[24] This effect is multiplied by the perception that others are likely to be honest, further encouraging trustworthy behaviour. Conversely, repeat encounters are less likely in a mobile society and the 'incentive to behave opportunistically is much greater'. Again, the 'Mutual perceptions that each has a greater incentive to cheat . . . promotes an atmosphere of distrust', stressing the systemic nature of trust levels.[25] To a considerable degree the issue of mobility exerts an influence on the further determinants of trust levels. Exploration of the relationship between mobility and trust in the Potteries will be based in a reconstruction of the business structure of the industry.

Secondly, Casson suggests that 'Time preference is important . . . because it affects an individual's attitude to a reputation for integrity'.[26] In other words, patience and the long view, both with regard to specific relationships and more generally, promote trust through rewarding good reputations. This issue will be explored through reference both to broad structural patterns and to the detail of inter-firm relations in the Potteries. Thirdly, it is postulated that trust is unlikely to flourish in a 'climate of anonymity in which everyone in a locality is a stranger-recently arrived, probably about to depart, and so "just passing through"'.[27] Such climates tend to be associated with high social mobility but can also be reinforced by wider cultural frameworks. Thus, the structural and behavioural patterns uncovered will be related to a national culture 'emphasising the negative aspect of freedom'.[28] However, this section will uncover considerable contradictions, the trade press of the pottery industry supported personal capitalism and independent manufacture in principle but condemned it in practice. Thus, we are led to Casson's final postulate; that a 'Moral unanimity based upon a shared commitment to basic values is important'.[29] Exploration of this issue will seek to uncover not only why firms were becoming less likely to trust each other but also the dimensions along which their value systems diverged or conflicted.

Casson's application of the notion of trust to the problems of markets and hierarchies is a reminder of the distinctly paradigmatic quality of the industrial district model, with the notions of trust and social embeddedness as some of its most salient characteristics. That industrial districts represent a neglected paradigm in the history of industrialisation, contrasted to both the hierarchical Chandlerian firm and the market, is explicit both in the work of Piore, Sabel and Zeitlin and of a number of influential historians. For Scranton, for example, the Philadelphia textile trades of the late nineteenth century represented a 'manufacturing system that stood as a fully realised alternative to the corporate industrial model . . . a mature "small business" alternative to industrial gigantism'.[30] However, if trust does not follow automatically from clustering then the status of the industrial district model may require review.

II

In considering the question of mobility we are primarily interested in one segment of the community in the Potteries, its businessmen and their firms. How stable and immobile was the business population of the district? This question will be addressed through a reconstruction of the structure of sections of the industry across three decades of the late nineteenth century.[31]

The demography of the Potteries in the late nineteenth century would suggest that this was a highly immobile society in which, therefore, we might expect to find relatively high levels of trust. The population of the Potteries was highly indigenous. There were, moreover, strong links between place of birth and occupation. Stated simply, potters were Potteries born.[32] Where the overall population of the district was highly immobile, however, its business population was commensurably fluid. This fluidity was to be found both in the aggregate and at the individual level. The principal impact of this fluidity was to generate economic and ideological tensions and distrust between large and small manufacturers, often overlaid with spatial and sectoral tensions and distrust between earthenware manufacturers in the north of the district and china manufacturers to the south.

A simple snapshot suggests some of the changes occurring in the business structure of the pottery industry in the second half of the nineteenth century. Table 4.1 presents a profile of the firm population of the central industrial and commercial town of Hanley in 1862 and 1882.

Immediately obvious is not only the overall growth in the number of firms but also an apparent growth in average firm size. Using Rateable Values as a proxy for the fixed capital assets of firms, these data would locate the typical firm in Hanley in 1882 in the medium-size category. Is this average typical though? In fact the typical firm remained small. Table 4.2 plots the size structure of the population of firms in Hanley in 1862 and 1882.[33]

Table 4.1 Pottery Firms in Hanley, 1862 & 1882

Year	No. of firms	Total RV (£)	Average RV per firm (£)
1862	40	4,241	106
1882	66	15,725	238

Source: Hanley Borough Rate Books, 1862 and 1882.

Table 4.2 Size of Firms in Hanley, 1862 and 1882

	1862		1882	
	No.	%	No.	%
Small	30	75	41	62
Medium	8	20	17	26
Large	2	5	3	4
Giant	0	–	5	8
Total	40	100	66	100

Source: Hanley Borough Rate Books, 1862 and 1882.

Clearly the small firm remained typical throughout this period, a point reinforced by evidence of falling levels of industry concentration.[34] By what mechanisms had growth in the overall size of the industry taken place? What were the individual prospects of the small firms that, as a class, continued to predominate? These questions can be answered by constructing a biographical history of the firm population under consideration. This is presented in Table 4.3.

Two features stand out: the mobility of firms in terms of their size and the relative instability of the small firm population. Both of these characteristics bear on the wider issues of mobility and familiarity as they relate to prevailing trust levels. Growth in the size of the medium, large and giant-size categories was fuelled largely or exclusively by the growth of firms. This point is reinforced if we consider the biographical history of the population of firms in Hanley in 1872 (see appendix A). Again entry firms made no contribution to the large and giant size categories. Of the five large firms of 1872, the pool from which three of the five giant firms of 1882 grew, four had displayed upward mobility from the medium size category between 1862 and 1872.[35] The one giant firm of 1872, Brown, Westhead, Moore & Co. (RV £1,524) had been a large firm in 1862 (RV £528).

Certainly the growth of firms, size mobility, is the not the same thing as social mobility.[36] However, in a national climate of laissez-faire political economy, the survival and growth of firms, demonstrated here and observable to contemporaries, served to legitimise and encourage the position and activities of smaller manufacturers, so widely viewed as untrustworthy and destabilising by large established firms and the trade press.

Table 4.3 A Biographical History of the Population of Firms in Hanley, 1882

Size

	Small		Medium		Large		Giant		Total	
	No.	%	No.	%	No.	%	No.	%	No.	%
Type of Firm Survival:										
Static	8	20	6	35	2	67	1	20	17	26
Mobile:										
Up	0	–	9	53	1	33	4	80	14	21
Down	0	–	0	–	0	–	0	–	0	–
All	8	20	15	88	3	100	5	100	31	47
Entry	33	80	2	12	0	–	0	–	35	53
Total	41	100	17	100	3	100	5	–	66	100

Source: Hanley Borough Rate Books, 1872 and 1882.

Independent, proprietary manufacture remained a seemingly practical aspiration for many skilled workers.[37] Recognising the validity and cultural context of that view, including not only the national framework but also the very strong local identification with potting as a way of life, serves to contextualise our later exploration of the lack of unanimity and commitment to shared values across the pottery industry as a whole.

Moreover, though size mobility need not lead automatically to social mobility, the growth of a firm was often accompanied by spatial mobility and organisational flux. A typical example is provided by the partnership of Wardle and Ash, which in 1872 was manufacturing parian statuary in a property owned by T. Randall on centrally located Broad Street, Hanley. This, like many parian shops, was a tiny concern with an RV of just £12. The firm did not appear in *Slater's Commercial Directory* of the town, published in the same year. By 1872 Wardle and Ash had separated, but both remained in business. George Ash was recorded in the Rate Books as being sole occupant of a rented factory on St. James Street with an RV of £33. *Kelly's* directory had him still making parian on Broad Street. That he was now trading as Ash & Co. suggests that another partnership had been formed to replace that with Wardle. Wardle had also acquired a new partner, though he appeared in the Rate Book as sole occupant of a rented works in Slippery Lane with an RV of £28. The 1860s had seen the survival of both men as manufacturers, though not without either physical or organisational upheaval, but little more. Their paths were to diverge in the following decade. Ash remained in the rented property on St. James Street, its RV growing to £44, perhaps through modest capital investment. He had once more dropped from *Keates' Directory* of that year. Wardle had, in comparison, prospered. Now in partnership with one D. Jones, he still occupied the small site on Slippery Lane, its RV having too grown, to £40. Wardle, however, also now owned a far more substantial factory on Victoria Road with an RV of £170. With a combined RV of £210 for the two works, Wardle and Co., manufacturers of parian and majolica, were a medium-size firm.[38]

The change in Wardle's station in life should not be underestimated. In twenty years he had progressed from marginal, artisanal manufacture, his and Ash's origins almost certainly being at the workbench, where they would probably have continued to work as fledging bosses, to the status and security of property ownership. More destructive of a shared climate of trust than the modest but solid progress of a man such as Wardle though was the constant instability of the small firm population. This instability was said to be result of the 'eager pressing into the position of manufacturers of men quite unfit for the position – unfit by reason of want of capital and of business acumen', and the 'unjustifiable intrusion of thoughtless men who aspire to be in business on their own accord'.[39] Whether aspirant capitalists deserved the opprobrium regularly heaped on them in the pages of the trade press is less important than the fact that they were perceived in this light. This was not the language of trust. As Staber notes 'if entry and exit are uncontrolled' then local networks 'are fluid and impossible to maintain'.[40] Casson makes a similar point, arguing that, 'The low-trust society makes adjustments through the birth and death of firms, and the relative growth and decline of the survivors'.[41] By analogy, therefore, the increasing rates of births and deaths in the Potteries in this period may be indicative of declining trust in a district exhibiting a Marshallian 'trees of the forest' growth pattern.[42]

The clear contribution of entry to the growth of the small firm population of 1882 is all the more remarkable given the considerable persistence of existing small firms. Seventeen, or 61%, of the twenty eight small firms of 1872 still existed a decade later, nine, 53% of surviving small firms also showed size mobility. However, despite these respectable levels of persistence and growth, surviving small firms are swamped by new arrivals in the pages of the 1882 Rate Books. Entry firms represented 64% of the small firm population in 1872 but 80% in 1882.[43] Attempts to link data in the Rate Books and Trade Directories serve only to emphasise this instability. Considerable numbers of firms appear in the Rate Books but not the directories, and vice versa. The majority of these were tiny, transient or both. Yet more appear in both, but with considerable variation in some detail, be it their name, production mix or location. In other words, neither Rate Books nor directories, published in the same year, were able to keep up with or agree on the composition of the town's shifting population of pottery firms. This situation was acknowledged at the time; 'We do not know how many are engaged in labour in the different branches of the trade. We do not know anything approaching the capital vested in the industry. We do not even know the number of manufactories or firms in the potteries of Staffordshire'.[44]

Again it is possible to trace some of the effects of these structural patterns at the micro-level. Sabel and Zeitlin claim, building on Scranton, that firms in nineteenth century industrial districts 'were not enduring units of production but rather temporary combinations of machines and skills directed at the achievement of particular tasks: the "constant" in the Philadelphia textile industry was the "mill building rather than the firm."'.[45] If so then attention to property rather than firms might allow us access to the constant tramp of start-ups and failures. A good example is a manufactory on Broad Street, Hanley owned by E. Bostock. In 1862 these works were occupied by the china manufacturing partnership of Rickhuss and Wilkinson (RV £77), in 1872 by Taylor and Tunnicliffe (RV £101), and in 1882 by Mary Massey, earthenware and figurine manufacturer (RV £142). Another example is provided by a works on Liverpool Road, Stoke-upon-Trent, owned by G. Turner and then by his executors. This 'potbank' was being worked by J. Stanway and Co., makers of china, earthenware and parian, in 1878 (RV £53), by earthenware manufacturers Shingler, Travers and Co. in 1886 (RV £57), and by J. Bevington in 1898 (RV £45).[46] With the exception of Taylor, Tunnicliffe and Co. it has not proved possible to trace any of these firms to any other locations at an earlier or later date. It is difficult to imagine that the majority of them had had time to develop significant reputations, either for their probity or for their wares.

Details extracted from reports of bankruptcies allow an appreciation of the marginal nature of these transient firms, encouraged into business by empty properties, the low capital intensity of a barely mechanised trade, a vigorous market in second hand plant and easily accessed local circuits of credit. If we add to these conditions the pressures of a highly seasonal trade then it becomes easier to understand both why these firms 'obliged to turn over money quickly . . . get so well patronised by the ready money dealers' and why they failed with such regularity.[47] As the *Pottery Gazette* noted in a laconic aside 'it is not at all wonderful that we have so many unsuccessful' firms.[48] Some of these bankruptcy reports make dismal and pathetic reading, with firms potentially imperilled by almost any exogenous shock. One such case was that of Daniel Cotton, whose bankruptcy was reported in June 1893. In the previous September he and Edwin Roberts had 'entered into partnership and commenced business at the Clayton Pottery. He invested £100 in the business, and Roberts brought in £45 with the intention of introducing more. On February 25 Mr Roberts met with a fatal accident, and a fortnight later the bankrupt closed the works, as he did not know how the business stood'.[49] The devastating impact of these failures on family economies cannot be doubted, equally important though was their impact on the tenor of the trade as a whole.

III

If the business structure of the North Staffordshire pottery industry was increasingly mobile and unstable at this time, is there any evidence of a rising incidence of untrustworthy or opportunistic behaviour? If there is, can this evidence be linked clearly to the structural patterns revealed above? If, as Casson argues, 'Repeat trading . . . is likely to be more common in a high-trust society' then, by analogy, a decline in repeat trading may be evidence of declining levels of trust.[50] Evidence drawn from the records of Jesse Shirley and Sons, processors and suppliers of bone and other inputs to pottery manufacture, will demonstrate that inter-firm relationships in the Potteries where characterised by a decline in repeat trading in the second half of the nineteenth century. To be sure, the pressure for this change came from the market place. Like many other industries, pottery saw the onset of increasingly difficult trading conditions from the late 1870s onwards. As the trade press observed, this 'great depression' was 'in value more than quantity.'[51] Nonetheless, falling prices were accompanied by increasingly erratic demand.[52] One moment observers seemed optimistic, with orders 'literally speaking, pouring in on every side', whilst at the next 'The whole commercial world, "Home" and "Foreign" seems paralysed to the core . . . We are face to face with a crisis in potting history'.[53] Similarly, larger 'respectable' firms could be working flat out before being suddenly deserted by buyers for the smaller firms. The result was that it was very often 'difficult to speak on the present state of trade with any confidence or reliability'.[54] This uncertainty was exacerbated by the tendency of buyers to demand ever longer terms of credit from manufacturers, placing increased pressure on the co-ordination of raw material sourcing, production and stock levels and on lines of credit. Manufacturers reacted to the increasingly contingent nature of the trade by 'working from hand to mouth'.[55] Pressure to adopt these strategies was clearly exerted externally, but the ability to adopt them was facilitated by and was only likely to further the falling levels of trust consequent upon the structural developments outlined above. How did these strategies manifest themselves in practice?

Shirley and Sons, formed as the partnership of Bourne and Hudson in the 1820, played an important role in the supply of materials to the pottery industry. Their principal trade was in ground bone, an important ingredient in bone china, and the firm was one of the first in the district to specialise in the processing and supply of this and other materials. By the mid-century the firm was well established and owned by Jesse Shirley, who had previously worked for Bourne and had married his widow on the death of his employer. In 1857 Shirley, whose older brother Joseph was a merchant trading in china clay from the south-west, expanded the firm's capacity by building a second mill. The firm's records for that year indicate a highly stable set of trading relationships at both the aggregate and individual level. The firm did business with a relatively small and very stable set of sources for raw bones and coal and with an equally consistent set of customers for the finished product. Moreover, within these sets, relationships with each individual firm varied little across time. Examples from the firm's customer base will illustrate these points. Between July and December the firm did business with nine local pottery firms. This seems a small number but the trade was highly dependable. Seven of these firms, distributed throughout the region but all concentrating on china manufacture, placed orders with great regularity. Typical was the Longton firm of Allerton and Co. who, with the exception of December, always placed between five and seven orders per month with Shirley. All of these orders were for 20cwt of ground bone. Shirley did not demand immediate payment. Thus, for example, the 220 cwt of bone delivered in 11 lots between 1 August and 26 September were paid for by Allertons with one bankers draft on 12 October. Though slightly less valuable, the pattern of trade with other firms, such as J. Lockett of Longton and Thomas Green of Fenton, was essentially the same. It is highly likely that for these seven firms Shirley was their only or principal source of ground bone, despite the presence of other potential suppliers in the district. They operated what would today be referred to as a preferred supplier sourcing strategy, rather than one of multiple or parallel sourcing.[56]

Certainly they do not appear to have used 'competitive discipline ruthlessly against their partner.' Casson suggests that in a low-trust climate firms will '"shop around" its partner's rivals, and use price comparisons to back up threats to switch trade away unless it gets a better deal'. There is no evidence that in 1857 Shirley's customers were making such switches 'purely to maintain the credibility of these threats'.[57] Conversely, the remaining two pottery firm customers each placed only one order with Shirley in the six month period analysed, suggesting that they too enjoyed stable relations with a preferred supplier and turned to another source, Shirley, only in exceptional circumstances. Firms seem to have sought and valued stability and loyalty in the district networks in which they participated. In turn the delayed payments they made reflected Shirley's trust in them.

By 1884 the situation was very different. We are interested here in identifying the nature of two sets of relationships. Firstly, there are those between Shirley and long-term customers, with whom it might be expected strong links involving notions of trust and reciprocity had been forged. Had these deteriorated? That Shirley, more than a quarter of a century later, still did business with firms, including Allerton and Co., that it had traded with in 1857 aids this enquiry. Secondly, focus will fall on firms whose relationships with Shirley were much newer, particularly those that can be identified as small new entrants to the industry.

Can particular forms of inter-firm relations be identified with such firms, linking such patterns to change in the structure of the industry?

The firm's customer base had certainly grown by the later date, but the fact that in 1882 the firm no longer occupied one of the three sites it had in 1872 suggests that this growth had not compensated for the increasingly erratic demands made by the district's manufacturers. Orders were patchy, often infrequent and generally smaller. Bone was also now ordered in many different, often fractional amounts (entirely unknown in 1857). Seemingly in response Shirley now also processed other materials and, perhaps most significantly, had begun to contract out its grinding capabilities. These changes in the day-to-day business activities of the firm may be related to two factors; that is to structural and strategic change in the wider industry. The latter point may best be seen in the change in the behaviour of established customers such as Allerton and Co. and T. and S. Green, china manufacturers of Park Street, Fenton. In 1857 both firms had placed only orders for 20cwt of ground bone at roughly one week intervals, the tempo of orders varying only slightly with the seasonal nature of the trade. In June 1884, however, Green, for example, placed only two orders, for 21 and 26 cwt of bone on the 9 and 19 respectively. Robinson and Son, china manufacturers of Sutherland Road, Longton and with whom Shirley had been trading since at least 1867, provide another example. They appear to have done a very vigorous trade with their supplier, placing 30 separate orders in June 1884 alone, but when that trade is examined in detail it is seen to be composed of a mass of petty transactions. They too now bought bone in amounts that were smaller than previously and fractional and the majority of their orders were for the grinding of very small amounts of glaze and colour. That long established customers behaved in this way is significant, suggesting that infrequent or irregular ordering was now the norm rather than the exception. Indeed, in 1884 most orders came from firms placing infrequent orders and most of the firms doing business with Shirley placed infrequent orders. Of the twenty-four pottery firms transacting with Shirley in June 1884, for example, 50% placed two or less orders and typically carried on in the same way throughout the year. Repeat trading was now less common, or certainly less reliable, strongly suggesting that switching was now taking place, manufacturers exercising competitive discipline as they themselves experienced fluctuating demand and falling prices. The trust which Shirley had established in the networks of the district could only do so much to override the imperatives of firms trying to reduce their costs and enhance their flexibility in an increasingly uncertain world.[58]

However, the rise of infrequent ordering amongst the majority of the firm's customers must be traced not only to change in the behaviour of established customers but also to the proliferation of small new entrants identified above. Shirley's records display a clear correlation between infrequent ordering and small new entrant firms, such as Banks and Thorley (RV £100) and E. Steel (RV £80), both of Hanley, or Shorter and Boulton (RV £83) of Stoke-upon-Trent.[59] These firms were typically placing one order a month with Shirley. Small new entrants were also more likely than older customers to place small orders or to need only the grinding of small amounts of glaze etc. Increasing mobility within the firm population of the industry, along with a quickening pace of entry and exit, had resulted in a decline in repeat trading and had, it may be surmised, emerged from and reinforced a growing climate of distrust.

IV

However, small new entrants behaved opportunistically not simply because of their mobility but also because of their time preferences. Their own marginal position and the pressures of an intensely seasonal trade gave them little opportunity to invest in the kind of time frame in which reputation might be recognised and developed as a valuable resource. Much of the pressure on these firms was economic. The *Pottery Gazette*, noting in 1885 that, 'Whilst some of the very best houses have been phenomenally slack, the small producers from one end of the potteries to the other, have been able to keep their ovens going', argued that this was because 'Most of them are obliged to turn over money quickly, and hence it is just now that they get so well patronised by the ready money dealers'.[60] However, in the following year, the *Gazette* explicitly bundled together financial insecurity, newness, and lack of reputation as characteristic of the typical small firm; 'Mushroom firms . . . having no good name to lose, and not much capital to lose either, are reckless in their dealings, caring only to send out something, and to get ready money for it quickly'.[61] To accuse someone of recklessness is clearly also to accuse them of being untrustworthy, in this case because they cared little for tomorrow. Their inability to nurture a reputation mattered because it was seen to impact on the reputation of the district as a whole; 'All this is very detrimental to the best interests of the trade, . . . depraving the taste of manufacturers, dealers and consumers alike'[62]

Of course small firms were not the only ones menaced by short-term pressures. It may have been true that the small manufacturer 'wants sovereigns at the end of the week. The getting of these to pay wages has ruined hundreds of small men', but in June 1894 the giant and venerable firm of Mintons, with a reputation matched only by Wedgwood, also found itself unable to pay its workers.[63] Mintons, however, had the financial and, above all else, cultural reserves to survive the crisis. Owner John Fitzherbert-Campbell, adding it to the debenture interest and rent he had already foregone, advanced £3,1000 to the struggling firm, which had been making losses since the mid-1880s. This response was typical of many made by the firm and its owners throughout this troubled period. Placing its faith in the value of reputation, Mintons drew deeply on the commitment of all involved in the firm, and in particular of family members. There can be no doubt that much of the strength of this commitment was derived from the age of the firm and from the fact that John Fitzherbert-Campbell represented the fourth generation of the family. Time frames at Mintons were long indeed, stretching from the past on into the future.[64]

If any small manufacturers did look beyond the next day or week they were perhaps more likely to aspire to a personal competence than to the construction of a dynastic firm. Scranton regards the notion of the competence as a 'phenomenon peculiar to . . . proprietary and partnership firms . . . one component of a culturally defined alternative to the corporate version of capitalism'.[65] However, the competence may also represent a defining difference between large and small firms within proprietary capitalism. Evidence suggests that the competence did figure in the aspirations of small new capitalists in the Potteries, and whilst it represented an extension to the very limited time frame of most small businessmen it also recognised that the multi-generational family firm, in which a premium was placed on reputation, was perhaps an unrealistic ambition. The *Gazette* certainly believed that desire for a competence was the motivation of many small capitalists:

> Almost every factory in Longton is 'bossed' by 'working men-masters'-men who, by dint of hard and unceasing labour, have left the bench for the counting house, the managers sanctum, or the flying visits of the 'commercial' . . . and so they go on jogging from day to day, seeing, perhaps, in the dim and misty future . . . a comfortable seat by the fireside devoid of every potting care.[66]

It was asserted that 'it is only in exceptional circumstances that the small capitalist or affluent artisan can by an investment of his savings in manufacture rise to a position of easy competence', but the reconstruction of business structure carried out above suggests there were still enough examples to encourage those willing to try.[67]

Scranton argues that in Philadelphia 'real estate and land purchases were an important element in building a competence', and interrogation of the Potteries' rate books provides tentative evidence that some may have followed this route in North Staffordshire.[68] One possible example is provided by William Warrington, who in 1862 owned and operated a very small earthenware manufactory on Brewery Street, Hanley (RV £14). By 1882 Warrington had retired, but he still owned the Brewery Street property, now occupied by parian and stoneware manufacturer J. Plant and yielding a gross annual rental of £59. More interesting is the case of William Harrop and T. Worthington. In 1862 this partnership was in business in a small way, the parian works that they jointly owned at Tinkers Clough, Hanley having an RV of £26. This situation remained unchanged in 1872, except that the work's RV had increased to £91, suggesting some investment. By 1882, however, both had retired. Harrop now owned an earthenware and parian factory at Mount Pleasant, Hanley, occupied by P. Bednall and C. W. Heath (RV £31). Worthington owned the adjacent site, occupied by J. Harrop and H. Hall, earthenware, parian and stoneware manufacturers, with an RV £132. It seems more than likely that J. Harrop was William's son and that the father's retirement had been recent, *Keates' Directory* of 1882 still recorded the firm as W. Harrop and Co. (As *Keates* also records both this firm and that of Bednall and Heath as being in Tinkers Clough it is probable that one of the two sites of 1882 was that originally occupied in 1862 and that the street name had simply changed).[69]

The example of Worthington and Harrop presents a complex picture of modest ambitions fulfilled and limits reached. The competence, with its medium time frame, placed a value on trustworthiness and reputation that fell somewhere between that of the many tiny transient firms and that of the long-lived, multi-generational family concern. However, modest though it was, it was position few attained. As the reconstruction of the business structure of the district has demonstrated, most small capitalists, though very probably Potteries born, were, as businessmen, strangers, 'recently arrived, probably about to depart, and so "just passing through"'.[70] They were, almost literally, anonymous, 'having no good name'. Was this individual anonymity situated in a wider culture of anonymity that, as Casson argues, was likely to further promote a growing climate of distrust?

Casson identifies high levels of anonymity with cultures which emphasise 'the negative aspects of freedom – the importance of maintaining privacy and tolerating nonconformity'.[71] If we add to these characteristics those of a high regard for the sanctity of property rights and for the individual over community and society it is possible to describe both late twentieth century America, as Casson does, and nineteenth century Britain as cultures 'liable not merely to condone anonymity but to promote it'.[72] Such attitudes would likely be corrosive of the community based moral economy posited by Sabel and Zeitlin.[73]

The *Pottery Gazette*, the principal trade journal of the industry in the last quarter of the century, certainly took a staunch, if highly conventional, line on matters of political economy. The Eight Hour Day movement, combative trades unions, factory legislation and government in general all received regular, withering blasts in its pages.[74] The journal also lent positive support to the notion of vertical mobility through personal endeavour and hard work, in principle at least. Thus, it was held that the 'most healthy form of work is what a man does on his own responsibility . . . Monster mills and gigantic concerns threaten to dissipate the useful middle class of comfortable and independent men'.[75] In the same vein, the rise of public limited liability companies was deprecated for their impact on the interests of privately held capital. Such beliefs could induce men such as William Woodall and Godfrey Wedgwood, neither of whom had ever been near a work bench, to claim that 'The people who do succeed in our business are men who have risen from the bench'.[76]

The impact of this ideology on the business community of the Potteries, particularly in terms of a culture of anonymity, may be discerned in the pages of the *Gazette* in several ways. Firstly, the editorial content of the journal was presented entirely anonymously. This policy was most significant with regards to the monthly Trade Reports. These, one for each township in the district, covered day-to-day commercial activity whilst also assessing prevailing attitudes and forthcoming developments. They also offered informed opinion and comment. The level of detail that they contained, in conjunction with their general tone, strongly suggests that they were written by people intimately involved in the industry, probably a large local manufacturer or, perhaps as likely, merchant. A similar blanket anonymity prevailed in printed correspondence. Letters were typically signed 'A Manufacturer' or 'An Earthenware Manufacturer'. Occasionally initials or the name of a township might be appended but never, in more than twenty years surveyed, did a manufacturer openly state his opinions in the pages of the *Gazette*. The individualism of personal capitalism was itself a force for secrecy and anonymity.

Such attitudes, however, penetrated deeper. Revealing is the correspondence of 'A Manufacturer' concerning a proposed alliance to raise earthenware prices in 1899. The writer began by affirming that, 'I would gladly support any scheme for securing an advance in the price of china and earthenware if anyone will submit one likely to secure that end. I do not associate myself with the present scheme, because I am quite sure that it can never have that end'.[77] The writer's scepticism, which proved well founded in this case, stemmed from a critique, steeped in laissez-faire doctrine, of the way in which the majority of manufacturers in the industry set their selling prices:

> Manufacturers instead of going closely into the question of the cost of production, have in scores of cases regulated their own selling prices by the prices charged by their competitors. This is the insanity of which I complain – the insanity which has been the cause of all the evil. There is only one sound business way, only one honest way of determining the selling price of an article you make. You must base it on the cost of production, and regulate it by the laws of supply and demand.[78]

Manufacturers, it was being argued, had no interests in common. Neither the clustering of the industry, leading to intense competitive pressures, nor any sense of collective identity or communal responsibility should have any bearing on prices determined properly by the costs of inputs and the impersonal mechanisms of supply and demand alone. In essence, the correspondent affirmed that all should, in Marshall and Farnie's words, 'undergo "the ordeal of economic freedom" within the open market'.[79] This freedom is clearly, in Casson's terminology, a negative freedom in which economic action is atomised, mechanistic and avowedly not socialised. The argument, displaying no 'solidarity sentiments', is an implicit rejection of the claim that the particular 'process of socialization' which takes place in an industrial district protects its 'economy as a whole against the consequences of short-term calculations of advantage'.[80]

No doubt the writer believed he was being rational, but to other manufacturers his stance may well have looked exactly like a mask for calculative opportunism. Under depressed trading conditions each vulnerable manufacturer felt that his own selfless action in pushing for higher prices would serve only to leave his business open to the predatory actions of others, thus he too would refrain from alliance and join those hunting for any order that could be secured. The result was a secrecy inimical to the openness required of successful alliance, as manufacturers repeatedly gave hidden discounts off published lists. This dilemma was expressed by 'An Earthenware Manufacturer' in 1891; 'the primary cause of failure in all past combinations of manufacturers has been in the fact of a few grasping manufacturers holding aloof and there by getting orders whilst those in combination have been positively without'.[81] It is quite clear that manufacturers in the Potteries could not trust one another and this distrust was, as Casson suggests, highly systemic in nature.

However, there are also clear indications that the *Gazette's* faith in the tenets of laissez-faire political economy, naturally privileging the aspiring, private individual over society, was beginning to weaken under a range of pressures. Not least amongst these pressures were the developments in the structure of the industry, and in particular the widening divide between large and small manufacturers, outlined above. These doubts were given vent in an explicit attack on the 'Smilesian ethic':

> The teaching of moralists who are forever holding up the mirror of success and pointing out the achievements of the few, has to a much larger degree than we should care to admit created an unrest in the ranks of labour which finds no remedy but in seeking to do as others have done, but under varying conditions – without thought of surrounding circumstances or even a shadow of success.[82]

The *Gazette* concluded by hoping that, 'before long things will revert to a position somewhat similar to that they used to occupy, and that the larger manufacturers will be those who alone will control the general spirit of the market'.[83] Underlying this hope was a belief that such a position was the right of larger manufacturers, perhaps even their moral right. Thus, we are led to examine Casson's final postulate, that trust levels within a culture will be influenced by the 'degree of unanimity in moral commitments'.[84] This issue will be explored via the story of The North Staffordshire Exchange. The failure of this body reveals not only the degree of distrust prevalent in the Potteries in the late nineteenth century, but also the dimensions along which large and small manufacturers differed in their moral commitments and values.

V

The complex story of the failure of the North Staffordshire Exchange demonstrates the difficulty of creating cohesion in a highly competitive industrial district, and is a reminder that the concept of the industrial district is as yet vague on the conditions under which effective levels of trust emerge and an optimum balance is struck between competition and collaboration. Further, the conflicting value systems of sections of the industry revealed in the Exchange can be related to the structural characteristics of the industry as shown above, that is to the mobility and instability of the business population of the district.

The North Staffordshire Exchange, projected and led by an industrial and social elite within the district and industry, existed for a few brief months in 1859 and then again between 1875 and 1882. The Exchange grew out of the North Staffordshire Chamber of Commerce, from which Longton firms, typically smaller than those in other parts of the district, already 'held aloof . . . under the impression that it was a clique of "large" makers on the "other side" simply to push their particular brands'.[85] The Exchange was intended, firstly, to facilitate the day-to-day business of the industry by providing a convenient and regulated location for the exchange of inputs and finished goods and, secondly, to promote greater unity in the industry through the exchange of ideas and the identification of common interests. Instead, it served largely to sow controversy and discord. The potential for discord was evident at an early stage. Supporters of association had high ideals. The Exchange would, it was hoped, be not only 'consecrated to the spirit of enterprise', but would also:

> prove a true mart of commerce . . . a temple of concord, equally sacred to the spirit of brotherhood, which shall animate those who have a common origin, common wants and an indissoluble mutual destiny; and a centre of intelligence from which shall go forth influences which shall quicken and reward legitimate emulation.[86]

At the same time, however, it was noted that these 'influences' were required in order to 'cause hurtful ignorance to disappear, and before which wilful prejudice and unholy jealousy shall expire'.[87] Thus, the example of the Exchange was to act to 'qualify individual assumptions, defeat and ring the knell of local . . . monopolies, and supersede local sectional ascendancies by the elevation of the whole'.[88] The motivations of the proponents of association can be traced then, at least in part, to an identification of the highly divided and competitive structure of the industry with negative effects on individual firms. However, the desire to instil greater cohesion in the industry clearly also required that the barriers to the realisation of that aim be acknowledged. Most significant though is the clear moral dimension to the language employed by promoters of the Exchange, echoing the wider attack on the behaviour and very existence of small capitalists noted above, which argued that small firms promoted an 'unhealthy competition' which ought to be subject to 'wholesome checks'.[89]

Central to the moral economy propounded by those involved in the Exchange, almost without exception the representatives of large multi-generational firms, were notions of legitimacy and fairness. On occasion the baser sentiments which lay behind lofty statements were made more explicit. Thus, in August 1859 it was noted that still missing from the Exchange were 'many of what Mr Grose . . . facetiously called "the dogs", but we suppose that we need not trouble about them, for if only the "hares" are there the dogs will most certainly follow'.[90] The "dogs" referred to small firms and the "hares" to older, larger and more 'respectable' houses, but the expression can only have served to further alienate the former from the latter and to heighten a pre-existing climate of distrust between the two. Indeed, both in 1859 and 1875–1882 the "dogs" refused to come in and both the general membership and, in particular, the Committee of Management of the Exchange remained heavily biased towards large earthenware manufacturers from the northern townships of Tunstall, Burslem and Hanley. The Exchange could not find the common ground on which to build an inclusive notion of 'the trade'. The unwillingness of the small firm sector, swollen during this period, to participate re-emphasises the role played by structural factors in the failure of the Potteries to generate either the enabling institutional framework or the high levels of trust posited by the industrial district model.

The drama and conflicts played out in the Exchange were situated within a wider debate about what it meant to be a 'true potter'. Again the emphasis in this debate fell on the issue of legitimacy. In a community so deeply immersed in pottery manufacture this was an issue important to all. The difficulty, and source of much conflict within the business community of the district, lay in deciding who were the real or true potters. Who most faithfully represented 'the Potteries'? Exogenous change played a role in heightening these debates. As Casson argues a low-trust culture will respond particularly badly when 'radical uncertainty prevails', as in a period of technological change and the internationalisation of markets.[91] Both of these conditions pertained in the pottery industry in the period under study. Thus, it was recognised in the late nineteenth century that:

> The tendency of the modern pottery manufacture is towards the more and more complete employment of mechanical devices to facilitate the production of and lower the price of various goods. The true potter will always be an artist, but the manufacturer, who caters for the greater number of people rather than the artistic few, will ever be driven to bow to the god of cheapness.[92]

However, external change acted only as a catalyst in the emergence of these tensions. Can these tensions and conflicts be usefully modelled? Prolonged and intense clustering combined with relative geographical,

political, cultural and even demographic isolation had led to the formation in the Potteries of what Massey calls 'deeply fundamentalist and
internalist' views of 'place and character'.[93] In such views people, indi-
vidually and, more especially, in groups, claim places for themselves.
They claim that they represent the essence of a place, or, in the language
of the *Pottery Gazette*, the 'spirit of the markets'. However, such views
typically fail to recognise that places are 'hybrid', the location of 'a mul-
tiplicity of readings'.[94] Moreover, the 'claims and counter-claims about
the present character of a place depend in almost all cases on particular,
rival, interpretations of its past'. These interpretations are in turn used to
'legitimate a particular understanding of the present (and) are put to use
in a battle over what is to come'.[95] Growing uncertainty over the future
in the Potteries in the late nineteenth century strengthened the need for
the legitimisation of conflicting views. Thus, the conditions which created a need for greater cohesion also made the engineering of trust more
difficult.

Using the understanding of place developed by Massey it is possible
to map the rival claims and value conflicts within the business community of the Potteries on which attempts to achieve a balance between
competition and co-operation foundered. Was the Potteries a place of
art or industry, of craft or mechanical manufacture, of independent men
or giant concerns, of fresh opportunities or established interests? All
these questions were vigorously debated by contemporaries and pola-
rised around the tensions and distrust existing between large and small
manufacturers. Increasingly, they placed damaging limits on the extent
of 'cultural consistency, normative backing and conformity to agreed-
upon-rule', from which, it is argued, a vitalising balance of competition
and co-operation should emerge in the 'ideal-typical industrial district'.[96]

VI

This exploration of trust levels within the Potteries industrial district
suggests conclusions in two areas. Firstly, growing levels of distrust
within the district may have had implications for the performance of
the industry in a critical period of emerging external challenge. Casson suggests that low trust impacts on performance by raising transaction costs in line with a perceived rise in the likelihood of others acting
opportunistically. Ultimately, a low-trust climate is likely to induce
internalisation in response to rising transaction costs, as transactors
taking 'the level of distrust in society as exogenous . . . seek out the
transaction cost-minimizing institutional response'.[97] However, in an

industry, such as that of the Potteries, with a structure of considerable vertical integration combined with intense horizontal fragmentation, the impact of declining trust was widened out beyond that on directly transacting firms. Declining trust exacerbated existing downward pressure on prices, intensifying local price competition and hindering collective responses. The district as a whole represented a 'slaughter-house', in which buyers were free to dictate prices.[98] Nonetheless, such was the comparative cost structure of the industry in North Staffordshire that falling prices were not sufficient to decisively beat the rising challenge of foreign competition, both at home and abroad. Inevitably profits were squeezed and firms failed. Given the reliance of the pottery industry on retained income as a source of capital investment a period of sustained low prices weakened process innovation in an industry already plagued by doubts about mechanisation.[99] The proliferation of small new firms, already the object of much distrust for their impact on prices, further weakened the response of the industry as a whole by inducing uncertainty in incumbent firms.

Significantly, however, uncertainty and price competition did not lead to a restructuring of the industry away from small-scale firms and intense horizontal fragmentation. The hostile conditions of the late nineteenth century purged many individual firms but they did not fundamentally alter the structure of the industry. The constant entry of new firms blocked the 'institutional response' of greater horizontal integration. Thus, in so far as growing distrust may be related to ease of entry and the consequent instability in the firm population of the industry, falling levels of trust occurred because of rather than despite the spatial clustering of pottery manufacture in an industrial district. A long history of spatial clustering had, by the mid-century, created in the region factor conditions and institutional infrastructures which supported a fragmented structure of many competing small and medium-sized firms. Those same conditions also allowed for the intensification of that structure in the period under study and sustained an individualistic personal capitalism as the characteristic organisational form of firms. The relevant conditions were, in simple terms, 'thick' supplies of physical and human resources. Important institutional structures included; cheap and accessible supplies of start-up and investment capital, equally cheap and accessible supplies of working capital, and networks of suppliers, buyers and agents, facilitating flows of information, materials and other commodities. These institutional frameworks were highly localised within North Staffordshire. These endowments and arrangements had three principal effects on the industry in terms of its structure; they made it easy to enter, they ensured a ready supply of new entrants and they aided the survival and growth of a proportion of those entrants.

Casson's exploration of the determinants of trust levels within a culture suggests that trust levels are systemic and this study has demonstrated that intense competition, falling levels of trust and a weak co-operative impulse in the Potteries were as much properties of the district as a whole as they were the result of the behaviour or attitudes of individual firms and businessmen. The fragmentation of the industry was reflected in a fragmented district-wide business culture inimical to the collective moral economy posited by Piore *et al*. Distrust between large and small firms, between the china and earthenware sectors, between north and south was clearly related to spatial clustering and increasingly placed limits on the cohesion of the district as a whole. These conclusions challenge the industrial district model to elucidate the conditions under which clustering will foster networks operating as 'high-trust mechanism(s) linking independent owners'.[100] If trust does not follow on automatically from clustering other attributes of industrial districts, including their resilience and flexibility, may also require further evaluation. However, this study does not invalidate the inclusion of socio-cultural as well as economic determinants in our analysis of the development of business networks, whether clustered or not. Indeed, it has the opposite intention. These socio-cultural factors seem likely, however, to show a high degree of place specificity. In this context Zeitlin's call for a move 'away from a "thick," "closed" model of the industrial district based on a stylised account of the Italian experience towards a "thin," "open" model capable of accommodating a variety of empirically observable forms' is to be welcomed.[101] He proposes a new model which 'would not assume that industrial districts . . . are necessarily innovative, flexible, consensual or otherwise successful'.[102] This work supports that argument and, by fruitfully exploring the *response* of a district to challenge, suggests that such a model might emerge from an evolutionary perspective on district development.

Notes

1 M. Piore and C. Sabel, *The Second Industrial Divide: Possibilities for Prosperity* (New York, 1984); C. Sabel and J. Zeitlin, 'Historical Alternatives to Mass Production: Politics, Markets and Technology in Nineteenth Century Industrialization', *Past and Present*, Vol. 108 (1985), pp. 133–176.

2 R. Lloyd-Jones and M. J. Lewis, 'Personal Capitalism and British Industrial Decline: The Personally Managed Firm and Business Strategy in Sheffield, 1880–1920', *Business History Review*, Vol. 68 (1994), pp. 364–411; C. Behagg, 'Mass Production Without the Factory: Craft Producers, Guns and

Small Firm Innovation, 1790–1815,' *Business History*, Vol. 40 No. 3 (July 1998), pp. 1–15: A. White '"We Never Knew What Price We Were Going to Have Until We Got to the Warehouse": Nineteenth Century Sheffield and the Industrial District Debate', *Social History*, XXII, 3 (October 1997), pp. 307–317.

3 J. Wolch and M. Dear (eds), *The Power of Geography: How Territory Shapes Social Life* (Boston, 1989).

4 U. Staber, N. Schaefer and B. Sharma (eds), *Business Networks: Prospects for Prosperity* (Berlin, 1996), D. Keeble and E. Wever (eds), *New Firms and Regional Development in Europe* (London, 1986).

5 Staber et al., *Business Networks*, p. v.

6 I. Taplin and J. Winterton, 'New Clothes from Old Techniques: Restructuring and Flexibility in the US and UK Clothing Industries', *Industrial and Corporate Change*, Vol. 4 Pt. 3 (1995), p. 618.

7 J. Melling, 'Review of C. Sabel and J. Zeitlin, Worlds of Possibilities: Flexibility and Mass Production', *Business History*, Vol. 40 No. 3 (July 1998), p. 175.

8 U. Staber, 'The Social Embeddedness of Industrial District Networks,' in Staber *et al.*, *Business Networks*, p. 148.

9 *Ibid.*, p. 157.

10 M. Casson, 'The Economics of Trust: Explaining Differences in Corporate Structures between the US and Japan', in M. Casson, *Enterprise and Competitiveness: A Systems View of International Business* (Oxford, 1990), pp. 105–124.

11 *Ibid.*, p. 105.

12 M. J. Stern, *The Pottery Industry of Trenton: A Skilled Trade in Transition, 1850–1929* (New Brunswick, 1995).

13 These differences are explored in some depth in B. Harrison, 'Industrial Districts: Old Wine in New Bottles', *Regional Studies*, Vol. 26.5 (1992), pp. 469–483.

14 R. N. Langlois and P. L. Robertson, *Firms, Markets and Economic Change: A Dynamic Theory of Business Institutions* (London, 1995), p. 125.

15 A. Marshall, *Trade and Industry* (London, 1919), p. 287.

16 *Ibid.*, p. 284.

17 *Ibid.*, p. 284.

18 U. Staber, 'Networks and Regional Development: Perspectives and Unresolved Issues,' in Staber *et al.*, *Business Networks*, p. 8.

19 Sabel and Zeitlin, 'Historical Alternatives,' p. 154.

20 M. J. Enright, 'Regional Clusters and Economic Development: A Research Agenda,' in Staber *et al.*, *Business Networks*, p. 201–2.

21 Harrison, 'Industrial Districts', p. 478.

22 Staber, 'Social Embededness,' p. 152. The place of trust within this argument is made explicit by Staber. Thus, echoing Casson, Staber claims that 'In time, recurring exchanges become increasingly structured and implicit rules for continued cooperation may emerge. The eventual outcome may be a network of individuals who are prepared to forego opportunities to abuse the trust bestowed upon them. Standard economic theory cannot account for such outcomes.' *Ibid.*, p. 156. Granovetter's original analysis also focused on trust; 'The embeddedness argument stresses . . . the role of concrete

personal relations and structures (or networks) in generating trust and discouraging malfeasance . . . continuing economic relations often become overlaid with social content that carries strong expectations of trust and abstention from opportunism'. M. Granovetter, 'Economic Action and Social Structure: The Problem of Embeddedness', *American Journal of Sociology*, Vol. 91 No. 3 (November 1985), p. 490.

23 Casson also argues trust is particularly important to highly disintegrated industries, typical of those found in industrial districts. He notes that it is 'evident that the ability to trust other people is especially important in simplifying strategic decisions relating to a production system which involves large numbers of linkages between different facilities. The more complex the division of labour that needs to be managed, in other words, the more important it is to have a high degree of trust to sustain it'. Casson, *Enterprise and Competitiveness*, p. 43.

24 *Ibid.*, p. 110 and p. 109.

25 *Ibid.*, p. 110.

26 *Ibid.*, p. 110.

27 *Ibid.*, p. 110.

28 This emphasis falls on, among other things, the 'importance of maintaining privacy . . . The culture of negative freedom tends to reduce the frequency of social interaction between people and to condone reticence in such interactions as do occur. It promotes anonymity and so discourages reputation building. This in turn leads to an atmosphere of distrust'. *Ibid.*, p. 110–111. This analysis clearly bears on the primacy of the individual and the sanctity of property rights within laissez-faire political economy.

29 *Ibid.*, p. 111.

30 P. Scranton, *Proprietary Capitalism: The Textile Manufacture at Philadelphia, 1800–1885* (Cambridge, 1983) p. 3.

31 This reconstruction is carried out using data extracted from the extant nineteenth century rate books for the Borough of Hanley, one of the six townships that made up Stoke-on-Trent and an important seat of pottery manufacture. The extant books are for the years 1862, 1872 and 1882. The rate books give a description of the property, its location, the owner and the occupier, the gross estimated rental and the rateable value (RV). Following the work of Lloyd-Jones and Le Roux, Lloyd-Jones and Lewis, Timmins and Lewis, RVs are used here as a proxy for the fixed capital assets of a firm. R. Lloyd-Jones and A. A. Le Roux, 'The Size of Firms in the Cotton Industry: Manchester, 1815–1841,' *Economic History Review*, Vol. XXXIII (1980); R. Lloyd-Jones and M. J. Lewis, *Manchester and the Age of the Factory* (London 1988); G. Timmins, 'Concentration and Integration in the Sheffield Crucible Steel Industry,' *Business History*, Vol. 24 (1982), pp. 61–78; M. J. Lewis, *The Growth and Development of Sheffield's Industrial Structure, 1880–1930* (Unpublished Ph.D. Sheffield City Polytechnic, 1989). For a fuller reconstruction of the business structure of the Potteries see A. Popp, *Business Structure, Business Culture and the Industrial District: The Potteries C. 1850–1900* (Unpublished Ph.D. Sheffield Hallam University, 1998).

32 In the important township of Burslem, for example, in 1871 just 5,064, or 19%, of a total population of 26,910 were not Staffordshire born. Only

2,032, a further 7.5% of the total population, of those born in the county of Staffordshire were born outside the city. In other words, over 70% of the population of Burslem were Potteries born. In fact the majority were Burslem born. Those born in other parts of the city were invariably from the adjacent townships of Tunstall and Hanley, incomers from Fenton and Longton at the southern end of the conurbation were rare indeed. Thus, this highly static society was in fact divided in ways likely to hinder interaction and trust. The links between place of birth and occupation were as strong as those between place of birth and residence. 6,553 of the largely native population of Burslem were directly employed in the pottery industry in 1871. This figure represents 24% of the total population and 51% of a working population of 12,916. *Census of Burslem*, 1871.

33 Size categories were constructed by plotting the total population of firms and mapping boundaries within that total. This process yielded the following scheme of categorisation.

Size Category (RV) (£)	Description
1–150	Small
151–500	Medium
501–1000	Large
1000+	Giant

For more details see Popp, *Business Structure*, Ch. 2.

34 Estimates of Industrial Concentration in Hanley, 1862–1882.

	% of 3 largest firm to total RV	% of 4 largest firm to total RV
1862	39	49
1872	33	41
1882	29	37

Source: *Hanley Borough Rate Books*, 1862, 1872 and 1882.

35 The fourth mobile giant firm of 1882, Clementson Bros. (RV £1187), had been a medium-size firm in 1872 (£458).

36 However, in an industry dominated by personal capitalism, in which owner and firm were closely identified with one another, business success and social mobility were strongly related.

37 This finding contrasts with Farnie's conclusion that in this period the 'cotton industry ceased to fulfil its historic function as a vehicle of social mobility'. D. A. Farnie, *The English Cotton Industry and the World Market, 1815–1896* (Oxford, 1979), p. 120.

38 *Hanley Borough Rate Books*, 1862, 1872 and 1882; *Slater's Commercial Directory* (1862); *Post Office Directory of Staffordshire* (London, 1872); *Keates and Ford's Directory of the Staffordshire Potteries and Newcastle* (Hanley, 1882).

39 *The Pottery Gazette*, May 1899, p. 551; *The Pottery Gazette*, December 1985, p. 1393.

40 Staber, 'Networks and Regional Development', p. 14.

41 Casson, 'The Economics of Trust', p. 117.

42 The rates of births and deaths in the small and medium-size categories in fact displayed complex and, at some points, conflicting movements. Comparing the periods 1862–1872 and 1872–1882 the small-size category saw a rise in the birth rate and a fall in the death rate, i.e. 64% of the small firms of 1872 were new entrants whereas 80% of the small firms of 1882 were new entrants, and 53% of small firms present in 1862 exited before 1872 and 43% of small firms present in 1872 exited before 1882. The medium-size category seems to have been under more pressure, comparing the same two periods the birth rate nearly halved and the death rate nearly doubled. In the Borough of Stoke-upon-Trent the period 1878–1886 saw an extremely high birth rate amongst small firms, 92% of small firms in 1886 were new entrants, and, relative to Hanley, a fairly low death rate, just 33% of small firms present in 1878 exited before 1886. However, the following period, 1886–1898, saw a dramatic increase in the death rate, 75% of small firms present in 1886 exited before 1898, that may be linked, it might be conjectured, to the very high birth rate in the preceding period. Thus, were the data available, it is possible that the high birth rate amongst small firms in Hanley in the period 1872–1882 resulted in an acceleration in the death rate in the next decadal period.

43 *Hanley Borough Rate Books*, 1862, 1872 and 1882.

44 *The Pottery Gazette*, September 1890, p. 818.

45 Sabel and Zeitlin, 'Historical Alternatives', p. 149.

46 *Hanley Borough Rate Books*, 1862, 1872 and 1882; *Stoke-upon-Trent Borough Rate Books*, 1878, 1886 and 1898.

47 *The Pottery Gazette*, December 1885, p. 1422.

48 *The Pottery Gazette*, December 1898, p. 1393.

49 *The Pottery Gazette*, June 1893, p. 535.

50 Casson, 'The Economics of Trust', p. 113.

51 *The Pottery Gazette*, January 1886, p. 40.

52 Witnesses from the Potteries giving evidence before the Tariff Commission of 1907 referred repeatedly to the uncertainty of demand they faced. Herbert Colclough, a Longton china manufacturer, for example, claimed that 'The continuity of employment and the amount of work in our trade and district is extremely irregular, and has been so for some years', *Report of the Tariff Commission: Vol. 5 The Pottery Industries* (1907), paragraph 141.

53 *The Pottery Gazette*, April 1883, p. 362; *The Pottery Gazette*, June 1883, p. 559.

54 *The Pottery Gazette*, February 1881, p. 159.

55 *The Pottery Gazette*, October 1883, p. 955.

56 Shirley, *Ledger*, 1857.

57 Casson, 'The Economics of Trust', p. 113.

58 Shirley, *Ledger*, 1884.

59 *Hanley Borough Rate Book*, 1882; *Stoke-upon-Trent Borough Rate Book*, 1886.

60 *The Pottery Gazette*, December 1885, p. 1422. Farnie too notes the pressures exerted on small firms in the cotton industry, arguing that 'fixed costs weighed most heavily on small producers . . . so that the factors facilitating access to the industry also encouraged unremitting production by existing manufacturers'. *English Cotton*, p. 192.

61 *The Pottery Gazette*, January 1886, p. 43.

62 *Ibid.*, p. 43.

63 *The Pottery Gazette*, December 1898, p. 1393.

64 For a fuller exploration of Mintons in this period see Popp, *Business Structure*, Ch. 5.

65 Scranton, *Proprietary Capitalism*, p. 70–1.

66 *The Pottery Gazette*, December 1881, p. 1052.

67 *The Pottery Gazette*, May 1884, p. 536.

68 Scranton, *Proprietary Capitalism*, p. 229.

69 *Hanley Borough Rate Books*, 1862, 1872 and 1882; *Slater's Commercial; Post Office; Keates and Ford.*

70 Casson, 'The Economics of Trust', p. 110.

71 *Ibid.*, p. 110.

72 *Ibid.*, p. 110.

73 Yasumuro claims that in a 'collective culture' such as Japan 'those who display a strongly individualistic attitude tend to be looked upon as egotistical and selfish, and despised by other members of society. In a working group, the person who has an excessively self-assertive personality often fails to form cooperative relationships with others and will find it difficult to gain sufficient support from his colleagues to achieve goals.' In other words, individualism obstructs consensus and trust and hinders group performance. However, as Yasumuro identifies entrepreneurship as 'dependent on a culture of individualism . . . in the Western sense,' this analysis poses questions for the Sabel and Zeitlin thesis of district collectivity. K. Yasumuro, 'Engineers as Functional Alternatives to Entrepreneurs in Japanese Industrialisation,' J. Brown and M. B. Rose (eds), *Entrepreneurs, Networks and Modern Business* (Manchester, 1993), p. 78.

74 For example, the *Gazette* argued that 'Once again has the soul of the meddler been gladdened by the introduction of yet another factory act', and urged all manufacturers to 'resist with all their might these repeated attacks on the liberty of the subject', *The Pottery Gazette*, May 1895, p. 349.

75 *The Pottery Gazette*, November 1889, p. 735.

76 *The Pottery Gazette*, May 1885, p. 560. Similarly, Farnie notes that 'a belief in the beneficial function of vertical mobility conformed to the ethos of liberalism and was especially cherished by members of the Manchester Exchange. It was however misleading in so far as it imposed a superficial Smilesian ethic upon a trade in which both success and failure were apportioned in flat defiance of rational expectation,' Farnie, *English Cotton*, p. 294.

77 *The Pottery Gazette*, February 1899, p. 81.

78 *Ibid.*, p. 81.

79 Farnie, *English Cotton*, p. 195.

80 Sabel and Zeitlin, 'Historical Alternatives', p. 154.

81 *The Pottery Gazette*, August 1891, p. 724.

82 *The Pottery Gazette*, May 1884, p. 536.
83 *Ibid.*, p. 536.
84 Casson, 'The Economics of Trust', p. 109.
85 *The Pottery Gazette*, January 1883, p. 60.
86 *The Sentinel*, 12 February 1859, p. 6.
87 *Ibid.*, p. 6.
88 *Ibid.*, p. 6.
89 *The Pottery Gazette*, October 1898, p. 1250; *The Pottery Gazette*, February 1888, p. 52.
90 *The Sentinel*, 12 February 1859, p. 6.
91 Casson, 'The Economics of Trust', p. 17.
92 *The Pottery Gazette*, July 1894, p. 575.
93 D. Massey, 'Places and their Pasts', *History Workshop Journal*, 39 (1995), p. 183.
94 *Ibid.*, p. 185.
95 *Ibid.*, p. 185.
96 Staber, 'Social Embeddedness', p. 169.
97 Casson, 'The Economics of Trust', p. 115.
98 The phrase was used by Farnie to characterise activity on the floor of the Manchester Exchange. Farnie, *English Cotton*, p. 192.
99 The effect of uncertainty in retarding capital investment was another constant refrain amongst Potteries' witnesses appearing before the Tariff Commission. Thus, Mr T. C. Moore, Chairman of the Parliamentary and Tariff Committee the North Staffordshire Chamber of Commerce and formerly of the giant Hanley firm of Brown-Westhead, Moore and Co., admitted that he had seen many continental factories that 'were of the very first rank', but went on to conclude that 'if we had the security they have there are plenty of people in our district who are prepared to furnish any amount of capital when they can see that it is going to be productive of good results'. *Tariff Commission*, paragraph 107.
100 M. Casson, 'Modelling Inter-firm Networks', *The Organization of International Business: Studies in the Economics of Trust Vol. 2* (Aldershot, 1995), p. 50.
101 J. Zeitlin, 'Why are there no Industrial Districts in the UK?' in A. Bagnasco and C. Sabel (eds), *Small and Medium Enterprises* (London, 1995), p. 100.
102 *Ibid.*, p. 100.

Appendix

Table A.1 A Biographical History of the Population of Firms in Hanley, 1872

Size

	Small Large		Medium Total		Large Medium		Giant Giant		Total Small	
	No.	%	No.	%	No.	%	No.	%	No.	%
Type of firm Survival:										
Static	10	36	3	30	1	20	0	—	14	32
Mobile:										
Up	0	—	4	40	4	80	1	100	9	20
Down	0	—	0	—	0	—	0	—	0	—
All	10	36	7	70	5	100	1	100	23	52
Entry	18	64	3	30	0	—	0	—	21	48
Total	28	100	10	100	5	100	1	100	44	100

Source: Hanley Borough Rate Book, 1872.

'Trust in an industrial district: The Potteries, c. 1850–1900'

A retrospect

'Trust in an industrial district: The Potteries, c. 1850–1900' was my first academic publication. It emerged from my PhD dissertation (Sheffield Hallam University, 1998) and was the first in a stream of publications on related topics that lasted for close to ten years and included monographs, books and journal articles, some of them co-authored with John F. Wilson and Steve Toms. Perhaps most significant of these publications was *Industrial Districts and Regional Business Networks in England, 1750–1970* (Aldershot: Ashgate, 2003), co-edited with John Wilson, which continues to attract citations today for its pioneering historical survey of English industrial districts. Of course, other business and economic historians, including Sheryllynne Haggerty and the late Francesca Carnevali, have also published on the topic of trust and social capital. Most recently Joe Lane has started pursuing a similar focus in his studies of the North Staffordshire Potteries in the period immediately preceding the one I was interested in.

The first thing that strikes me on rereading the piece for the first time in a number of years is how much it is of its time, particularly in the way it seeks to build itself on a foundation in economics (and the work of Mark Casson in particular). This was very typical of British business at the time and it does allow me to build and then test a number of propositions quite effectively, drawing on a surprisingly wide range of quantitative and qualitative data. However, this way of working also led me into some traps. In particular, though I seek to problematise other accounts of the determinants of levels of trust in industrial districts, what I never do is question the central concept of trust itself. An understanding of trust is assumed. Obviously that is not satisfactory in either a conceptual or a methodological sense, but it also suggests an underlying bias towards the economistic. Today, I would be much more interested in interrogating trust as a social and cultural construct.

But the article shows fledgling signs of that interest in the one thing that it definitely does well, which is to place a very firm interest on, first, issues of industry structure and, second, industry culture, acting on one another in dynamic tension. That model, once scaled up, was able to generate some important insights into district life cycles, particularly as they enter into phases of decline. Reconstructing industry structure as concretely as possible proved to be very important to generating those insights. In that sense, I am very pleased to see that Joe Lane is applying a similar lens to the preceding period in the history of the North Staffordshire Potteries. Intriguingly, Joe's preliminary findings suggest the need for further refinements. Thus, during earlier periods of crisis, such as the Napoleonic Wars, he observes the industry responding by reducing the number of new entrants, whereas I observed an increased flow of new entrants during periods of crisis in the later nineteenth century. The obvious inference is that the dynamic between structure and culture plays out differently at different phases of the district life cycle. It is exciting that we still have much to learn about this important topic.

Index

Note: numbers in bold indicate a table. Numbers in italic indicate a figure.

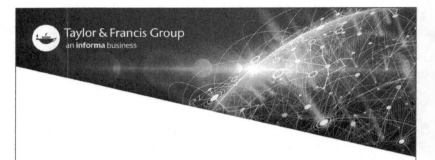

Printed in the United States
by Baker & Taylor Publisher Services